Design and build in timber frame

J. Burchell
F. W. Sunter

Design and build
in timber frame

Longman
Scientific &
Technical

Longman Scientific & Technical
an imprint of
Longman Group UK Limited
Longman House, Burnt Mill, Harlow
Essex CM20 2JE, England
Associated companies throughout the world

First published 1987

British Library Cataloguing in Publication Data

Burchell, Jim
    Design and build in timber frame.
    1. Wooden-frame buildings – Great Britain
    – Design and construction
    I. Title II. Sunter, F. W.
    721'.0448   TH1101

ISBN 0-582-30157-2

Set in 10/11 pt Linotron 202 Plantin Roman
Printed and Bound in Great Britain
at The Bath Press, Avon

Contents

Foreword

This book is intended to provide a guide for designers, builders and supervisors of timber-framed houses and small commercial buildings. In essence the method of building is simple and the construction of the frame is well within the capabilities of any reasonably well-qualified carpenter. It is the most commonly used form of low-rise construction in the developed countries of the Western world and the techniques of providing comfortable, safe, durable and economic structures have been proved many millions of times in every conceivable climate. Notwithstanding this fact, as timber frame has become more widely used in the UK almost every facet of the method has been further researched in the field and in the laboratory, and this has resulted in the adoption of standards for timber-framed construction which, in many instances, are higher than anywhere else in the world. The UK requirements for engineering design certificates, the National House Building Council (NHBC) architect appraisal certificate and the extensive use of preservative treatments are to a large extent peculiar to this country.

This book covers UK practices and reflects the fail-safe approach to timber frame construction which has been adopted.

Acknowledgements

We are grateful to the following for permission to reproduce copyright material:

British Gypsum Ltd for extracts from the *British Gypsum White Book*, and for our Figs. 3.8–3.24 inclusive; Cape Insulation Ltd for our Figs. 3.6 and 3.7; Gee, Walker and Slater Ltd for our Fig. 3.1; Potton Ltd for our Figs. 8.6 and 8.7; Wates Built Homes Ltd for our Fig. 1.2.

Chapter 1
Introduction

The history of timber frame building in Britain is as old as the history of building itself. As in most countries throughout the world, timber was the first construction material to be used for permanent buildings and there are many examples of timber frame buildings still performing their original function and dating as far back as the twelfth century. By the end of the sixteenth century the building method was quite well formalized. It consisted of a series of transverse posts and beams formed from large sections of hardwood which were assembled on the ground and tilted up into position. Lateral beams were then installed to support the floor joists and the rafters. The method tended to discourage any irregularities in the plan shape but it was common practice to construct overhangs at the front and rear upper floors using shorter timbers for the posts and simplifying the joints at intersections. The external wall frames were originally infilled with wattle and daub and subsequently by timber and brick. At a later stage in the development lighter vertical member and timber claddings were introduced. This was the method of building which was exported to North America along with the first settlers.

The colonists found an abundance of raw material suited to their needs though in the early days they had neither the time nor the money to indulge themselves in the intricate external decorations of Elizabethan architecture. The heavy frame construction coexisted with the Scandinavian log construction until the nineteenth century but neither method could satisfy the needs of a rapidly expanding population. The introduction of steam-powered sawmills made the production of smaller timber sizes more economic and the invention of the wire nail as a method of jointing timber provided a basis for a new technology of light timber frame building. The first recorded structure to be built with 2 × 4 in. framing timber was St Mary's Church in Chicago in 1830, and it was referred to derisively as balloon frame construction. As a building method light timber framing evolved rapidly and within a short space of time was adopted universally across the continent for all low-rise construction. The term 'balloon frame' is still used where the studs run full height from the sole plate to the eaves but it has been superseded by the use of storey-height studs in the platform frame method as detailed in this publication. Platform frame simplified fabrication and erection by using shorter pieces of timber but it was originally adopted because it minimized the occurrence of shrinkage defects occasioned by the necessity at that time to use unseasoned timber.

The exterior finishes were for the most part horizontal weatherboards though brick veneer was used in the more prosperous and developed urban areas. As in many Victorian houses the internal finish was wood lath and plaster which adapted readily to the dimensional irregularities of the timber framing. When high-speed planing machines were introduced into the sawmills early in this century builders were quick to recognize the advantages of working with accurately dimensioned timber, and timber planed all round is standard for all structural uses in North America. Gypsum lath replaced the old wood lath and was used until after the Second World War when gypsum wallboard began to be used for wall and ceiling linings. At the same time plywood bonded with a weatherproof glue was introduced and quickly supplanted boards as a wall, floor and roof sheathing material.

When timber frame house construction migrated back across the Atlantic to the UK the platform frame method was being used in North America to build over 1 million houses a year in every conceivable climate. Although there was an infinite variety of design and finish the construction details were remarkably consistent. Surfaced and stress-graded timber used in conjunction with 4 ft. 0 in. by 8 ft. 0 in. sheets of exterior grade plywood for sheathing and 4 ft. 0 in. wide gypsum boards for internal lining were to provide a modular discipline which would adapt ideally to British requirements. Up until the mid-1950s there had been only a limited number of timber-framed houses built each year in the UK, mostly imported from Canada or Scandinavia, or produced here by the early pioneers of timber frame such as W. H. Colt of Bethersden and Guildway. Because of limited knowledge and usage of timber frame the level of acceptance in the building by-laws, by insurance companies, building societies and the general public was virtually zero. It was in this climate that the Canadian Government and the forest industry embarked on a campaign to encourage the reintroduction of timber-framed housing to Britain. Display homes were built at several exhibitions which aroused great interest but no significant progress was made on the promotional front until two factors combined to ensure future success.

The first was the disastrous winter of 1962–63 which made people painfully aware of the fact that the climate could be less than temperate and that there was merit in having adequate insulation and heating systems typical of North American and Scandinavian timber frame construction. The second factor was the Government's resolve to provide more new housing and to encourage industrialized systems as a means of increasing production. An interchange of technical missions was sponsored by the Canadians and after seeing at first hand the comfort, quality and economy of Canadian houses the British mission of 1963 led by Sir Donald Gibson, Director-General of the Ministry of Public Buildings and Works, concluded that timber frame was a building method suited in every way to British requirements. The need for better thermal insulation, using a proven method of building with component manufacture off site to provide safe, comfortable and economic housing could be satisfied by using this form of construction. In 1964 three pairs of houses were built to demonstrate the technique followed by a council development of 183 houses in Harlow in 1967. By this

Fig. 1.1   Terrace timber frame housing, 1968

Fig. 1.2   Timber frame housing for private development, 1983

time a number of British specialist designers, fabricators and builders had adopted the Canadian timber frame method and were already in production.

Almost two-thirds of the houses being built were for local authorities who were under pressure from the Government to use industrialized systems. Most of the systems, and there were over 400, were for pre-cast concrete high-rise buildings and have since fallen into disuse and on occasion disrepute. To obtain local authority contracts timber frame builders also had to have a system, a factory and an appraisal certificate from the National Building Agency. This naturally led to the adoption of the use of factory-fabricated components in contrast to Canadian practice where even today most houses are framed up on the site. In Britain the skilled labour for this operation was not available, giving a

further impetus towards the use of factor-made components which has been maintained till the present time. By and large all timber-framed systems are based on Canadian platform frame construction and differ only in minor details.

The growth of the timber frame sector of the housing market was steady if not spectacular until 1978. By this time fundamental changes had occurred to the pattern of housebuilding. The balance had swung away from the public to the private sector and the building of high-rise blocks for council tenants virtually ceased altogether. Although there was a drop in the overall number of housing starts the concentration on building low-rise dwellings left plenty of scope for timber frame. The energy crisis was with us and the need for improved thermal performance was recognized, but perhaps the most significant factor was in the housing market itself. With a decline in sales and relatively static prices it was no longer viable for developers to complete houses and wait for buyers. The speed of timber frame construction attracted major builders to the North American alternative which is to open a development with attractively decorated and furnished show houses and then to build against confirmed sales. As a consequence the developer has the minimum amount of capital tied up in unfinished or unsold houses and the reduction in site labour associated with the use of factory-fabricated components facilitates adjusting output to demand.

The lead given by the major housebuilders was followed by smaller ones and by June 1983 timber-framed houses in the private sector constituted almost one-quarter of the total starts though the percentage has slipped back since then. To what extent the method will replace brick and block in the future is a matter of conjecture. What is not a matter of conjecture is that timber frame has a proven record in Britain as in many other countries of providing well-built, safe, comfortable and economically operated houses. As a method of construction it is attractive to developers and builders and as home-owners gain confidence in its benefits it should gain a very substantial share of the housing market.

Timber frame methods

Timber frame house construction methods fall into three broad categories listed in their ascending order of importance, namely balloon frame, post and beam and platform frame. Elements of one form of construction may be incorporated with another providing that the designer understands the techniques and characteristics of both and the ways in which they interact.

Balloon frame

As noted earlier, balloon frame was the first form of light timber framing to be used in North America and it enjoyed a very brief period of popularity in Britain in the 1960s. The studs on external walls are full height from the sole plate to the roof with the intermediate floor joists supported on noggings let into the studs. As shown in Fig. 1.3, blockings are required to provide the necessary fire stops to floor and wall cavities. The method does not adapt readily to prefabricated building techniques due to the size and weight of two- and three-storey-high panels and the difficulty of erecting them.

Problems occur when joists shrink as they dry down to their equilibrium moisture content. Since there is virtually no shrinkage in the full height external wall studs, cracks in the internal finish are common at the junction of partitions supported on joists and external walls. Similarly cracks can develop where ceiling linings are attached to clear span trusses. These are some of the reasons why the balloon frame method is rarely used.

Post and beam

This method which was in a sense the original form of timber construction came back into fashion in North America in the 1950s mainly as the prerogative of architects designing individual houses rather than merchant builders or developers. Some impetus was provided by an increase in the availability of glued laminated timber which allowed the designer to specify members of almost any size or length. Apart from having a better structural performance than solid timber, glued laminated timber made from small sections of kiln-dried timber does not develop the shrinkage nor seasoning defects which almost invariably occur as large sections of timber dry down to an equilibrium moisture content.

Post and beam construction (see Fig. 1.4) is essentially a structural grid of beams supported on posts usually on a regular spacing of between 2 and 5 m which is an economic distance for spanning secondary roof and floor members of solid timber. The modular spacing gives a strong sense of rhythm and discipline

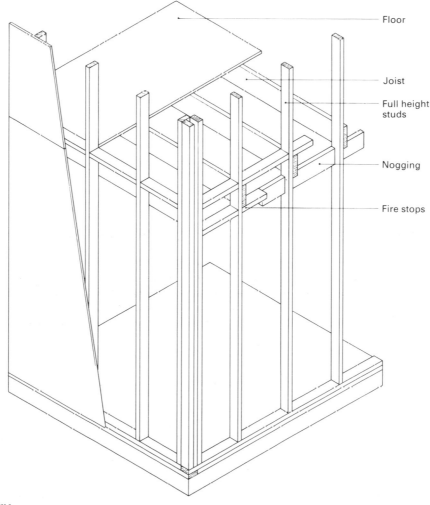

Fig. 1.3 Balloon frame

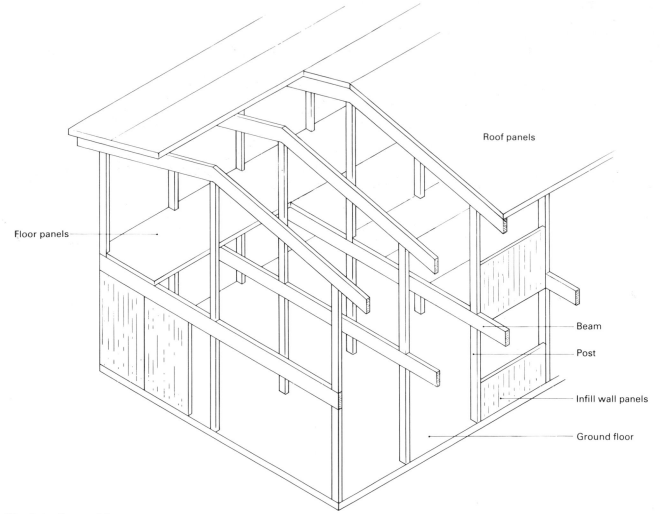

Fig. 1.4   Post and beam

to both the plan form and the elevations, the main structural members being exposed and emphasized. The post and beam framework is stabilized by the infill panels which form the walls, floor and roof. For the walls these may be of conventional non-load-bearing stud construction or alternatively sandwich panels with a foamed polyurethane core lined internally with plasterboard and externally with a suitable weatherproof cladding such as plywood providing that the component achieves adequate resistance to racking. Similarly floors and roofs can incorporate conventional joists and rafters or alternatively prefabricated stressed skin plywood panels can be used.

The structural concept does impose some design restrictions but because of the strength of the main members it provides opportunities to cantilever floors and roofs beyond the limits which can be achieved with other methods of construction. Post and beam houses can be built on conventional foundations, but since the whole of the structure is supported at a limited number of specific points the foundation can consist of pads or posts which can be a real economic advantage on difficult sites.

Platform frame

This is the method of timber frame building most widely used in North America and almost exclusively in Britain. It derives the name from the fact that each floor is built as a platform which extends to the exterior

face of the external walls. Starting with the ground floor walls and partitions, of single storey height, which may be site-built or prefabricated in a factory, are erected, plumbed vertical and fixed into position. The first-floor joists are then installed on top of the ground-floor panels and when the structural floor deck is in place there is a strong, safe working platform on which to erect the next storey-height set of walls and partitions (see Fig. 1.5). It should be noted that where the structural flooring material is less weather resistant than exterior quality plywood it should not be installed until the structure is weathertight and the advantage of the working platform is then lost.

Platform frame offers infinite flexibility to the designer and provides the builder and prefabricator the opportunity to vary the size and degree of factory content in components to suit their particular requirements. While there are some variations in material specifications, the main difference between competing platform frame 'systems' is in the type of component and how far down the way towards a fully factory finished unit the manufacturer has gone. The steps on the way may be described as follows.

1 All timber members and sheathing are pre-cut by the supplier and delivered for assembly on the site. In North America this is called stick-build.

2 The wall components are framed up in the factory with the sheathing applied to external walls. The components are storey height and the maximum

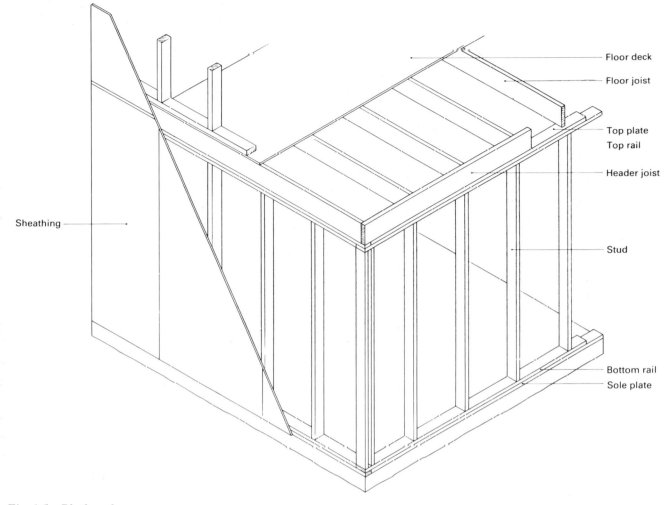

Fig. 1.5   Platform frame

length is predetermined by the manpower available on site, e.g. 2.4 m for a two-man erection crew. The roof trusses are supplied factory fabricated and as in stage 1 the joists and flooring are pre-cut to size. External joinery may be included in the panels or supplied separately.

3   Each storey-height component is fabricated full length usually with window and door joinery installed. The floor may also be divided into panels for factory fabrication along with the roof trusses. At this stage and those following a crane is required for site erection (see Fig. 1.6)

4   This is similar to stage 3 with the addition of glazed windows, doors and insulation. Depending upon the material specified external finishes may be applied, and also plumbing, wiring and internal finishes, thus forming in effect a sandwich panel.

5   This stage involves the factory fabrication of fully finished volumetric units. They are transported to the site, set on prepared foundations and when the site joints between units and service connections have been made are virtually ready for immediate occupancy. This stage may be delayed by the installation of external finishes such as masonry.

The demarcation lines between the various stages of fabrication are not sharply defined and any stage may incorporate elements from another. A good example might be where standard kitchen and bathroom layouts with a high degree of labour content are factory fabri-

cated into volumetric units and used in conjunction with a panel system.

It is essential that the designer is aware of the restrictions which begin to apply beyond the second stage of prefabrication which is the point at which crane handling of components apply. There must be site access both for the larger components and the crane and because crane handling is so rapid it is usually not economic for individual dwellings, but only where a number of house shells are to be erected at the same time. The use of factory-produced volumetric units imposes additional limitations on the designer who must take into account the size of unit which can be transported and handled on site. A further consideration is that it is unlikely to be economically viable for a factory to produce a limited number of volumetric units, a reasonable production run is therefore essential.

From the foregoing it is apparent that for the foreseeable future timber frame house design will be based on the assumption that the small-panel system will be used and the designer can utilize all the freedoms of building in timber.

Design considerations

Designing a timber-framed house requires many of the same disciplines as designing for other methods of construction in order to achieve the time-honoured objectives of 'commodity, firmness and delight'. Once a conscious decision has been taken to build in timber

Fig. 1.6   Erection of large components using crane

frame there are certain differences from brick and block construction which should be recognized if full advantage is to be taken of the building method. In the heyday of council housebuilding it was not unusual for local authorities to go out to tender on documents which left the choice of construction method to the contractor and resulted in look-alike houses which did not reflect the merits of any method of building. Timber frame because of its lightness and strength has the great advantage of flexibility in plan form and cross-section. Long spans, large openings, cantilevers, set-backs and complex plan forms are easily achieved and economically built. In this context the designer should note that some of these advantages could be negated if masonry veneer is used exclusively as the exterior finish and that other lighter-weight materials such as timber, tile hanging and stucco should receive due consideration where their use is appropriate.

To a degree timber frame is a modular concept in terms of design. Sheet materials, usually 1.2 by 2.4 m in dimension, are used for floor decks, wall sheathing and interior wall and ceiling linings. To accommodate them, studs, joists and roof trusses are spaced at 300, 400 or 600 mm centres with a major grid of 1.2 m (Fig. 1.7). Recommended practice is to locate the grid line on the exterior face of the studs to suit both the wall sheathing and the floor deck, i.e. the more expensive sheet materials.

Some systems show the major grid line located on the interior face of the wall. Packing pieces are required under wall components resulting in discontinuity of the floor diaphragm. Additional packing pieces are also required at corners and partition junctions, complicating both the fabrication and the erection sequence. This practice is not recommended.

Slavish adherence to the concept of modular design in determining the external dimensions of the frame does not produce any significant economies particularly in one-off designs, since the supply of the external wall frames represents only a small percentage of the total cost of construction. As Fig. 2.7 shows, in any length of wall only one stud spacing needs to be non-modular.

All internal partitions, both load-bearing and non-load-bearing, may be located according to planning requirements with no reference to the module, but as previously stated the accurate modular spacing of studs, joists and trusses must be adhered to in order to accommodate the jointing of sheet materials.

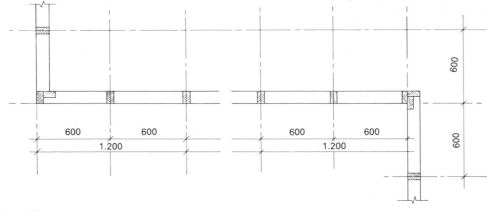

Fig. 1.7   Modular grid

Building Regulations

The Building Regulations 1985 (England and Wales) are compiled as a set of functional requirements with which a building and its elements must comply. Schedule 1, Parts A to L specify these requirements and practical guidance on complying with them is given in a series of approved documents. With the exception of the mandatory rules for escape in case of fire, there is no obligation on the part of the designer to adopt any particular solution in these documents providing that it can be shown that the requirement can be met satisfactorily in some other way. Although this apparently provides an opportunity for innovation and inventiveness it should be noted that if a contravention of the regulations is alleged, then if the guidance in the document has been followed, this will be accepted as evidence of complying with the regulations.

The Building Regulations for Scotland are in the process of being amended for the purpose of correcting errors or omissions and to update references to British Standards and Codes of Practice. While there are some differences in the regulations between England and Wales, Scotland and Northern Ireland their purpose is the same – to ensure that buildings are built to be safe, durable and comfortable. In the case of timber frame housing, it is also the purpose of this book.

Structure

Approved document A–A1/2 Loading and ground movement

The building shall be so constructed that the combined dead, imposed and wind loads are sustained and transmitted safely to the ground without such deflection or deformation as to impair the stability of the building or any adjoining properties or result in the building's failure to meet other requirements of the regulations. A further requirement is that the building shall be so constructed that movements of the subsoil caused by swelling, shrinkage or freezing will not impair the stability of any part of the building. In the case of timber frame these requirements are met because structural calculations for each house must be carried out by a competent professional engineer in accordance with the BS 5268 : *The Structural Use of Timber*. The approved document provides span tables for certain timber members but it should be noted that the sizes have not been regularized in accordance with standard timber frame practice. These calculations are required by both the local authority and the NHBC.

Fire precautions

Approved document B–B2/3/4 Fire spread

There is a requirement to ensure that a safe means of escape is provided in three-storey houses or flats. This may be met by complying with the requirements of the regulations 'Mandatory rules for escape in case of fire'. This document refers back to BS 5588 : *Fire Precautions in the Design and Construction of Buildings* : Part 1. *Code of Practice for Single Family Residences* and to the BS CP 3 Chapter IV. *Precautions against Fire*, Part 1 : 1971. *Flats and Maisonettes (in blocks over two storeys)*. In general terms this requirement can be met in single-family three-storey houses by providing a stair-case enclosed by full half- hour fire-rated partitions with the access doors self-closing and in the case of ground and first floors also fire-rated. In three-storey flats stair-cases should be enclosed by one-hour fire-rated partitions with self-closing fire-rated doors. In flats the walls to stairs and corridors would generally be compartment or separating walls having the required one-hour fire resistance. Although it is not a mandatory requirement where access to flats is from an enclosed corridor it is good practice to provide a means of escape at both ends of the corridor.

Internal fire spread (surfaces). Regulation B2

In order to inhibit the spread of fire within the building, materials used on exposed finishes on walls and ceilings shall be reasonably resistant to the spread of flame and if ignited shall not have an excessive rate of heat release.

Generally internal surfaces of walls and ceilings will meet this requirement with a Class 1 spread of flame rating, Class 3 being permitted for the ceilings in single-family one- and two-storey houses. Class 3 is also permitted for part of the wall not exceeding 50 per cent of the floor area nor 20 m^2. In timber-framed housing the linings will normally be gypsum wallboard which has a Class 0 spread of flame rating. Timber, plywood or chipboard chemically treated with a fire retardant or an intumescent paint to provide a Class 1 rating can be used providing that the wall or partition has the required fire resistance.

Internal fire spread (structure). Regulation B3

The requirements of the regulations are that:

1 The building shall be so constructed that in the event of fire its stability shall be maintained for a reasonable period.

2 The building shall be divided into compartments where it is necessary to inhibit the spread of fire within the building.

3 Concealed spaces within the building shall be lined and subdivided where it is necessary to inhibit the unseen spread of fire and smoke.

4 Semi-detached or terraced houses shall be separated by walls which offer a reasonable degree of resistance to the spread of fire and smoke.

These requirements may be met by using the following guidelines. External walls and load-bearing partitions in houses up to three storeys and flats up to two storeys should have a minimum half-hour fire resistance. Intermediate floors in two-storey houses should have a minimum of a modified half-hour fire resistance. The intermediate floors in three-storey houses and two-storey flats should have a minimum half-hour fire resistance (one hour for flats in Scotland). Three-storey flats should have a minimum one-hour fire resistance for external walls, load-bearing partitions and compartment floors. Separating walls and floors between houses and flats up to three storeys may be of timber frame construction. The designer's attention is drawn to the fact that any floor with a required fire resistance must be supported on walls or partitions with equal or better fire resistance.

Concealed cavities, which must be stopped around the perimeter area, are limited as to their maximum dimension by the nature of the material lining the cavity. In the case of timber-framed external walls and floors one side of the cavity will be a combustible material such as plywood and the maximum dimension allowed is 8 m. In walls the fire stopping is provided by the plates which are an integral part of the construction and in the floors by the header joists and the solid blocking provided between the joists. Standard construction details also satisfy the requirement that concealed cavities in elements should not interconnect, e.g. floor and wall elements. Contrary to standard practice in other countries, the same criteria are applied to the cavity between the brick veneer, which is a non-structural, decorative, weather-resistant cladding, and the load-bearing timber frame element. Fire stopping at party wall junctions and around openings is necessary but horizontal fire stops at each floor level are open to question since the floor and wall cavities in the elements of construction are already fire stopped and the vertical dimension does not exceed 8.0 m.

External fire spread. Regulation B4

The external walls and roof of a building shall offer adequate resistance to the spread of fire from one building to another. Recommendations for meeting these requirements are covered fully in the approved document and suitable cladding materials are governed to a large extent by the size of the building and its distance from the relevant boundaries. Where the building is 1 m or less from the boundary a minimum fire resistance of one hour is required with non-combustible claddings. As the distance from the boundary increases the area of the wall designated as unprotected increases. Unprotected area is defined as window, door or other opening; any part of the wall with less than the required fire resistance; any combustible cladding more than 1 mm thick. Where any part of the wall is unprotected because of the use of combustible cladding the unprotected area shall be deemed to be half the area of that cladding. The approved document with formulae and tables explains how to calculate the allowable percentage of unprotected area in any circumstance and also provides a simplified table (table 1.1) applicable to small residential buildings.

This section of the Regulations imposes restrictions on the choice of external cladding materials in terms of their combustible and non-combustible claddings to obtain the best aesthetic appearance (see also Ch. 6 – Claddings).

Roofs

Roof surfaces are classified in terms of fire penetration from the exterior and as to surface spread of flame and

coded for both with two letters A to D in descending order of performance in accordance with test results to BS 476 : Part 3. National designations of various roof coverings are given in Appendix A to the approved document B. Most of the more common roofing materials such as concrete tiles can be used without restriction but special attention should be paid to the more exotic materials such as cedar shingles and thatch where a distance of 12 m from the boundary is usually required.

Garages

In England and Wales a small garage (up to 40 m²) may be attached to the house providing the following conditions are met:

1   The timber floor over and the walls between the garage and the house must have full half-hour resistance.

2   Any door connecting with the house must have half-hour fire resistance opening out from the garage with a self-closing device.

3   A minimum step up of 100 mm from garage to house. The requirements in Scotland are most stringent where the fire resistance between garage and house is increased to one hour.

Site preparation and resistance to moisture

Approved documents:
C1/2/3 Site preparation and contaminants
C/4 Resistance to weather and ground moisture

The requirements of regulations C1/2/3 are that the ground to be covered by the building should be reasonably free from vegetable matter and contaminants and that subsoil drainages should be provided where necessary. Regulation C/4 requires that the walls, floors and roof of the building shall adequately resist the passage of water to the inside of the building. Recommendations for meeting these requirements are given in the document and fully covered in this book in Chapter 3.

Regulation DI – Cavity insulation

This requirement applies to insulation inserted into the cavity between the two leaves of a cavity wall. It is not applicable to timber frame construction where this type of cavity fill should not be used in any circumstances.

Regulations E1/2/3 – Airborne and impact sound

Approved document E

This requirement states simply that separating wall should have a reasonable resistance to the passage of sound and that separating floors should have in addition a reasonable resistance to impact sound. The document shows recommended methods of meeting these requirements and provides a table of acceptable sound transmission values. The details of timber-framed separating walls and floors covered in Chapter 5 of this book are based on both laboratory and field tests and consistently perform better than the Regulations require.

Table 1.1   Approved document B2/3/4 of Building Regulations

Minimum distance between side of building and boundary (m)	Permitted unprotected areas in small residential buildings	
	Minimum length of side (m)	Maximum total area of unprotected area (m²)
1.0	24	5.6
2.5	24	15
5.0	12	No limit
6.0	24	No limit

Regulations F1/2 – Means of ventilation and condensation

Approved document F

These two regulations require that there shall be an adequate supply of air provided for people in the building and that reasonable provision should be made to prevent excessive condensation in roof voids above insulated ceilings. These requirements may be met by following the relevant recommendations of BS 5925 : 1980. *Code of Practice for Design of Buildings: Ventilation Principles and Designing for Natural Ventilation* and BS 5250 : 1975. *Code of Basic Data for the Design of Buildings; the Control of Condensation in Dwellings.* Alternatively the designer may follow the recommendation in the approved document F. These are that ventilation to habitable rooms, kitchens and bathrooms should be in the ratio of 1/20 of the floor area with some part 1.75 m above floor level. Additionally roof voids above insulated ceilings should have the equivalent of 10 mm ventilation running the full length of the eaves for roof pitches over 15° and 25 mm for roof pitches under 15°. Where the insulated ceiling follows the pitch of the rafters 50 mm of space must be left between the top of the insulation and the roof sarking.

The control of condensation in the roof space should be automatic providing that the vents are not blocked by insulation but the control of surface condensation within the timber-framed house as with any other house depends upon the occupier utilizing the means of ventilation provided (see Ch. 3).

Approved documents G, H, J, K

These documents cover the regulation requirements for hygiene, drainage and waste disposal, heat-producing appliances, and stairways, ramps and guards which are common to all forms of construction.

Conservation of fuel and power

Approved documents:

L2/3 Resistance to the passage of heat

L4 Heating system controls

L5 Insulation of heating services

It is only the requirements of Regulation L2 which are of particular relevance to timber frame construction. This clause requires that in dwellings the calculated heat loss through windows and roof-lights shall be no greater than it would be if the aggregate of their area was 12 per cent of the area of the walls surrounding the building and the U value was 5.7, i.e. single glazing. A further requirement is that the calculated rate of heat loss through the solid parts of the exposed elements should be no greater than if the exposed walls and floors had a U value of 0.6 and the roof a U value of 0.35.

To the extent that the calculated heat loss through the walls and roof can be reduced by improving the insulation the areas of windows and roof-lights may be increased. Double and triple glazing will also permit an increase in area and the document provides examples of the calculations required. Since the U value of a timber-framed wall with 80 mm insulation and brick veneer is approximately 0.4 W/m² °C the designer has somewhat more flexibility than with typical block construction. By increasing the width of the studs to 150 mm and filling the stud cavity with insulation the U value can be lowered to 0.25 allowing further flexibility in fenestration. It should be noted that the cladding materials used have only a minor effect on U values when compared to variations in thickness of the insulation. In some buildings such as narrow-fronted terrace houses the window areas can be critical if sufficient light and ventilation are to be provided and the use of wider studs with additional insulation might well be adopted as a general principle.

Breather papers and vapour barriers

Breather papers were introduced to the UK along with modern timber frame where they were used both as a second line of defence against wind-driven rain and snow which could penetrate timber or stucco claddings. They also served as temporary weather protection while the site-built house was being built and sometimes in the case of self-build operations this could be a considerable time. The use of breather paper behind a brick veneer exterior is a much less critical operation since any water which might penetrate the cavity will first of all meet weatherproof WBP (Weather and Boil Proof) plywood and beyond that treated timber. It is specified by most designers and as such must be properly applied in accordance with the methods outlined in this book. The most critical factor is that while it prevents solid moisture from penetrating from the outside it is vapour permeable, allowing water vapour which escapes from the inside or which is residual in the timber to dissipate to the exterior. Breather papers are covered by BS 4016 but reference should be made to the NHBC Practice Note No. 5 which requires a higher quality of paper.

Vapour barriers or vapour checks as they are more properly called are designed to restrict the passage of water vapour under pressure into the external elements of the building. They are usually polythene sheet materials and the subject is covered more fully in Chapter 3. A flow of air through an opening in the internal lining will permit the passage of vapour much more readily than any defect in the vapour barrier itself. The designer is reminded of the fact, though he should not rely on it, that the Gyproc linings will have a coat of sealer, in itself a partial barrier, and in high humidity areas a finish of ceramic tiles, vinyl wallpaper or gloss paints. In other words not just one but three vapour barriers.

Timber and timber-based material

This section describes only those structural materials which are particularly relevant to timber construction and where applicable the British Codes and Standards are referenced. Those materials which are common to other methods of construction such as bricks and gypsum wallboard are not covered in this section.

Structural timber

Virtually all of the structural timber used is imported, the principal sources of supply being Scandinavia and Canada. Since a timber-framed house is an engineered structure it follows that the timber used must be stress graded. Because the construction is precise it also follows that the timber must be accurately dimensioned and close to its equilibrium moisture content at the time of erection. Permissible stress values for various grades and species are tabulated in BS 5268 : Part 2. *The Structural Use of Timber*. Three principal grading rules are covered; BS 4978 : *Timber Grades for Structural Use*; the National Lumbar Grading Authority Rules for Dimension Lumber, Canada NLGA rules; the National Grading Rules for Softwood Dimensioned lumber, USA NGRDL rules. It should be noted that the Canadian and United States grades are for all practical purposes identical.

Timber may be graded to the BS 4978 rules either in Britain or the country of origin, both Scandinavia and Canada being sources of supply. Timber graded to foreign grading rules such as NLGA and approved for use in Britain may only be graded in the country of origin.

Grades

There are four basic grades listed in BS 4978. In ascending order of strength they are as follows:

General Structural: GS visually graded or machine graded MGS
M50 Machine graded

Select Structural: SS visually graded or machine graded MSS
M75 Machine graded

The Canadian and American grading rules are somewhat more complicated since they take into account both the size of the timber and the end use. The grades and sizes commonly imported are shown in Table 1.2.

In addition to the various grades available there is a number of species or species groups. European redwood/whitewood, spruce–pine–fir and hem–fir from North America, southern pine from the United States, each group having different strength properties for the same timber grades. In BS 5268 an attempt has been made to simplify the specification of structural timber by introducing the concept of strength classes. For structural softwoods these range from SCl to SC5, each class having a specific set of permissible stresses. If the designer uses these values in the engineering design then any grade and species combination allocated to the

strength class specified can be used in the construction. Table 1.3 shows some of the more widely used grades and species and their appropriate strength classes. All structural timber should carry a stamp showing the grade, grading rule, and identifying the authorized grader or grading agency. North American grade stamps also identify the species group and a number identifies the mill at which the timber was produced.

When specifying timber either by strength class or by grade it should be noted that there are variations between the natural characteristics of different species in respect to dimensional stability, treatability with preservatives, appearance, etc., which will influence the specifier.

Timber sizes

The British Standard BS 4471 : Part 1. *Dimensions for Softwood, Basic Sections*, lists the sizes of timber that are available, including those from Canada planed all round to Canadian Lumber Standards (CLS) dimensions. The standard also tabulates the reductions in the basic size of sawn timber which is permitted when it is processed by regularizing or planing to ensure that the timber is dimensionally accurate. Although any timber above the minimum size of 60 × 38 mm may be stress graded and used for structural purposes, in practice only a limited number of sizes and grades are used. There are shown in Table 1.4 at a moisture content of 19 per cent.

Moisture Content

Unseasoned timber may have a moisture content in excess of 100 per cent expressed as a percentage of the weight of the moisture to the weight of oven-dried wood fibre (see Appendix 1). When the free water in the cells of the timber is all dispersed, at around 30 per cent the fibre saturation point is reached. As the timber dries below this point it will shrink in width and thickness but in most species not noticeably in length. This shrinkage averages about 1 per cent for each 4 per cent drop in moisture content. Given that the equilibrium moisture content in service may be around 15 per cent

Table 1.2 NLGA and NGRDL grades, uses and available sizes

Grade	Recommended uses	Sizes (mm)	Length specification (mm)
Light framing Construction	Load-bearing walls and partitions	38–100 thick 38–100 wide	1.800–4.800 and longer
Standard	Non-load-bearing walls, noggings, etc.		
Structural light framing Select structural	Where higher strength is necessary, e.g. 'W' trusses	38–100 thick 38–100 wide	1.800–4.800 and longer
No. 1 and No. 2	General construction uses, principally wall framing		
Structural joists and planks Select structural	Where higher strength is necessary, e.g. beams and lintels	30–100 thick 114 and wider	1.800–4.800 and longer
No. 1 and No. 2	General structural use, e.g. joists and Rafters		

Table 1.3 Softwood species/grades combinations which satisfy the requirements for strength classes

Standard name	Strength class for BS 4978 grades				
	SC1	SC2	SC3	SC4	SC5
British grown					
Douglas fir		GS	M50/SS		M75
Larch					
Scots pine			GS	SS	
			GS/M50	SS	M75
Imported					
Redwood/whitewood			GS/M50	SS	M75
Spruce–pine–fir			GS/M50	SS/M75	
Hem–fir			GS/M50	SS	M75
Douglas fir–larch			GS	SS	
Southern pine			GS	SS	
	Strength class for NLGA and NGRDL grades				
	SC1	SC2	SC3	SC4	SC5
Spruce–pine–fir			No. 1, No. 2	Sel.	
Hem–fir			No. 1, No. 2	Sel.	
Douglas fir–larch			No. 1, No. 2	Sel.	
Southern pine			No. 1, No. 2		Sel.

Table 1.4 Timber sizes

Basic British sizes
Thicknesses (mm) 38, 44, 47, 50, 63, 75
Widths (mm) 75, 100, 125, 150, 175, 200, 225, 250, 275, 300
Notes: 1 Reduction in basic size for regularized timber:
3 mm for timber up to 150 mm
5 mm for timber over 150 mm
2 Reductions in basic size for planing dry timber:
3 mm for timber up to 100 mm
5 mm for timber 100 mm to 150 mm
6 mm for timber over 150 mm
3 Timber over 225 mm wide is most likely to be imported from North America
North American sizes
Available graded to NLGA or NGRDL rules
Width (mm) 38
Thicknesses (mm) 63, 89, 114, 140, 184, 235, 286
Notes: The sizes shown are for timber planed all round at 19 per cent moisture content

there would be a 3 per cent shrinkage factor if the timber was installed at or above the fibre saturation point. It is worth noting in this respect that edge-grained or vertically grained timber shrinks much less than flat-grained timber.

Ideally all timber components should be fabricated, erected and kept at a moisture content close to that at which they would stabilize in service. With standard forms of construction this is an impossible ideal in the British climate, so it is necessary to effect a reasonable compromise. This is to use timber dried to 19 per cent moisture content and to ensure that components delivered to site are under roof as quickly as possible. Excess moisture content is not a problem in terms of structural durability as it would have to remain above 22 per cent for fungal attack to occur, and timber frame is so engineered as to allow any residual moisture to migrate to the exterior and in addition external wall components are pressure treated with preservative.

However, excessive shrinkage in studs will cause cracks to appear at the joints between the gypsum board and internal second fixings which would have to be made good. It is essential that all wall framing should be below 19 per cent moisture content before the dry lining is installed.

Choice of timber

While certain regional preferences exist for timber supplied from one source or another it is advisable to allow the fabricator or supplier some degree of flexibility so that he will have the opportunity to obtain suitable timber at the most economic price. To a large extent grades and sizes will be determined by engineering calculations but the designer should bear in mind that these are not the only parameters which determine the size of timber to be used. Framing members must be thick enough to accommodate joints in the gypsum board, and as Fig. 1.8 shows, a minimum thickness should be 38 mm. They must also be wide enough to

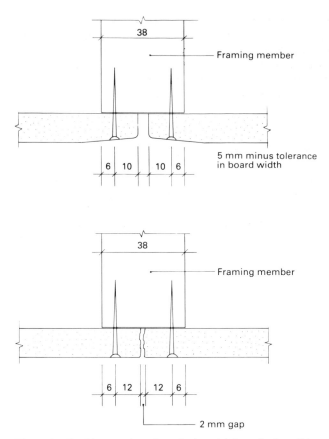

Fig. 1.8   Backing to plasterboard edges (a) bound edges (b) cut edges

accommodate the thickness of insulation specified and also any services which are located within the cavities in the framing. Where framing members are notched or drilled beyond the limits shown in Chapter 3 either an increase in size or suitable reinforcing is required.

Wall, floor and roof sheathing

The designer has a number of materials which may be specified for sheathing, particularly for walls. They range from structural softwood plywood to low-density asphalt-impregnated fibreboard, each with its own characteristics. Any material chosen should have a proven record in service and a known structural performance. Acceptable softwood plywoods are listed in BS 5268 : Part 2 and include Canadian, American, Swedish and Finnish, the principal sources of supply being Canada and America. All plywood should be manufactured with a fully weatherproof glue so that there is no possibility of delamination either during construction or service.

Plywood is available in 1200 × 2400 mm sheets and thicknesses from 7.5 to 20.5 mm in grades suitable for the intended use. When it is fixed to wall, floor or roof framing, the frames become rigid diaphragms capable of resisting the racking forces imposed by wind loads or seismic disturbance and prevents dimensional distortion during transport and erection. The plywood also provides temporary weather protection and in the long term an effective barrier to the movement of air through the external fabric of the building.

Since plywood wall sheathing is invariably covered the grade is specified for performance and not for

appearance, the Canadian grade being sheathing and the American either CCX or CDX. Knots, knot holes and other growth characteristics are permitted in the face veneers to an extent that does not affect the structural performance.

Medium-density fibreboard, tempered hardboard, chipboard and asphalt-impregnated fibreboard are also used as wall sheathing though to a lesser extent than plywood. Their structural properties in terms of racking resistance are given in BS 5268 : Part 6 and when specified it is recommended that advice on their application should be obtained from the appropriate trade association listed in Appendix 2.

Floor sheathing

Although it is possible for the floor sheathing to provide both the structural deck and the finished floor it is standard practice to cover it with a finish such as tiles or carpet. Panel materials such as plywood or chipboard are generally preferred to softwood boardinq since they lend themselves more readily to the modular concept of timber frame and the limited number of cracks provide a more acceptable substrate for most flooring finishes. A higher grade of plywood is required than for wall sheathing and is usually specified as select sheathing tight face for Canadian plywood or filled and touch sanded for American. Both of these grades have all open defects filled and are available tongued and grooved (T & G) on the long edges to eliminate the need to provide blocking. The plywood from whatever source should carry a stamp clearly indicating the grade, the species, the national production standard, and the use of an exterior quality glue. Canadian plywood will have a Council of Forest Industries (COFI) stamp indicating Douglas fir plywood manufactured to CSA 0121 or Canadian softwood plywood manufactured to CSA 0151. American plywood should carry an American Plywood Association (APA) stamp showing that it has been manufactured to the National Product Standard. Full information on these plywoods is available from COFI and the APA.

Where chipboard is used it should be specified as being manufactured to BS 5669 and should also carry a stamp indicating this fact and also the type of chipboard. Type II chipboard used for flooring has improved strength qualities and Type II/III has in addition improved moisture resistance. It is recommended that Type II/III is specified for all flooring applications in timber-framed housing. Chipboard is somewhat more susceptible than plywood to dimensional changes due to variations in moisture content especially at the edges. It should be installed after the house has been made weathertight and if necessary conditioned to approximately its equilibrium moisture content. It can be supplied with T & G joints on all edges and care should be taken in handling and installation to protect these edges.

Roof sheathing

Apart from the special requirements of the Scottish Building Regulations in respect to solid sarking, sheathing is not normally required under conventional roofing materials such as terracotta or concrete roofing tiles. In North America where the most commonly used finish of pitched roofs is asphalt shingles, plywood roof sheathing is used to provide a solid deck on which to fix the shingles and at the same time to brace the roof structure and thus reduce the requirements for internal bracing. In the UK roof sheathing is primarily used as the structural deck in flat and low-pitched roofs to receive a built-up felt and gravel roofing. In a timber-framed house with either a cold or warm roof deck only a fully exterior grade plywood sheathing should be specified. The appropriate grade should be Canadian select sheathing or its equivalent for conventional flat roof finishes and this should be upgraded to select sheathing tight face where roofing with a single-layer membrane is specified.

Fastenings

With the exception of the fixings used for the sole plate and the use where appropriate of joist hangers and truss clips for the roof structure, the structural joints in timber frame are made with nails. Nailed joints are strongest when the load is acting at right angles to the nails and in timber frame virtually all nails are so stressed. Common wire nails are usually specified but annular ring or otherwise deformed nails can be used to advantage in unsheathed components as an aid to keeping the joints tight during transport and erection. In general terms nails should be twice as long as the thickness of the timber member at the joint, e.g. a 38 mm plate being fixed to a stud requires 75 mm long nails. There is no structural advantage in increasing the number, length or diameter of the nails but there is a distinct possibility that in doing so the timber members will split and the effectiveness of the joint will be reduced. A full erection-nailing schedule is shown in Chapter 7, p. 60.

Chapter 2

Elements of construction

Footings and foundations

As with other forms of construction, the regulations require that the building should be so constructed that the combined dead, imposed and wind loads are transmitted safely to the ground and that movements of the subsoil caused by swelling, shrinkage or freezing will not impair the stability of the building. The depth and width of the footings are thus determined in theoretical terms by the loading, the nature of the foundation material and the climate. Practical considerations such as the width of excavation in which a bricklayer can work may affect the width of strip footings which are usually around 700 mm wide. For all except the worst soil conditions this should be sufficient to support brick-veneered timber-framed walls up to three storeys high.

Designers should take advantage of the lighter weight of timber frame and alternative details to reduce the cost of foundations. For example, trench fill foundations may be used in firm or sandy clay, the concrete being poured into a neatly excavated trench, and in most situations not having to exceed 350 mm in width. Figures 2.1 and 2.2 show typical foundation details.

A very important consideration, particularly in relation to the use of prefabricated components, is that the foundation wall or slab at sole plate level should be dimensionally accurate, true to line and angle and dead level. The accuracy with which components are fabricated demands similar standards from the bricklayer or concretor since there are very limited opportunities to correct discrepancies once the sole plate is positioned and firmly fixed. With either a suspended timber or a

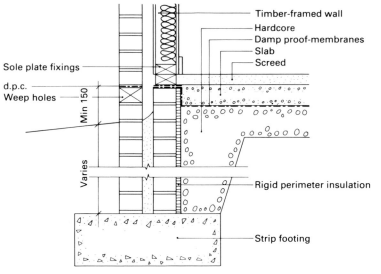

Fig. 2.1 Concrete slab on grade

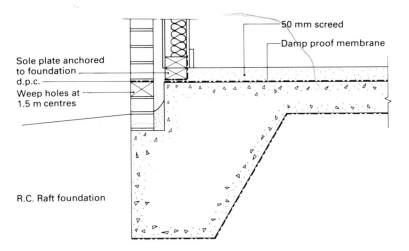

Fig. 2.2 Raft foundation

solid concrete ground floor the first element of the timber frame structure to be installed is the sole plate. This is usually the same width as the studs with a nominal thickness of 50 mm and pressure treated with a copper chrome arsenate preservative. An approved damp-proof course (dpc) is installed under the sole plate and where a cement screed is to be applied to the top of the slab the dpc should be turned up on the inside of the plate and stapled to it. The plates should be set dead level using shims or a mortar bed. Where shims are used any voids beneath the sole plate should be packed solid with a cement/sand grout. The NHBC specifies a maximum mortar bed of 20 mm and also that the plus or minus tolerance of the plate relative to the edge of the foundations does not exceed 12 mm. The plate is securely anchored to the foundations in accordance with the structural engineer's design requirements. A variety of methods are used including bolts preset in the concrete, rag bolts or expanding bolts, steel pins cartridge-fired into the concrete or preset fixing blocks in masonry, and proprietary fixings such as 'U'-shaped galvanized metal anchors set in masonry or shot fired to concrete. In most cases these fixings will perforate the dpc, but years of experience both in Britain and abroad have provided no evidence that this constitutes a problem. It is interesting to note that in Canada there is no requirement for preservative treatment nor even a dpc providing the plate is more than 150 mm above the finished grade.

Internal sole plates are placed and protected in a similar fashion to those in external walls. There are no engineering requirements in respect of the number of fixings but they should be located at approximately 1.2 m centres with a minimum of two to each length of plate.

Ground-floor construction

In addition to the requirement for structural integrity the Building Regulations further require that the floor should adequately resist the passage of moisture from the ground to the interior of the building. In the case of a concrete slab on grade there are two principal methods of meeting this requirement and on some difficult sites both methods may be used as a form of insurance. One is to install a well-lapped sheet of damp-proof membrane laid on hardcore which has been blinded with sand before the slab is poured. Where possible this membrane should be interconnected with the dpc under the sole plate. The other method is to apply two coats of emulsified asphalt on top of the slab underneath the cement and sand screed.

The concrete slab has been the most widely used ground-floor construction, south of the Scottish border, for the last forty years and it is certainly the most economic solution on a relatively flat site with good soil conditions. It is debatable whether it is either economic or desirable on a sloping site or one with poor soil conditions where a suspended ground floor may provide a better solution. The NHBC requires that where the depth of fill exceeds 600 mm a concrete slab should be designed as fully suspended spanning between bearing walls and suitably reinforced. There are a number of proprietary systems of pre-cast concrete joists with block infills available to provide a concrete floor without the requirement for fill.

Another solution is to use a suspended timber floor which would seem logical in the context of building a timber-framed house. The use of timber floors under the 1976 Building Regulations was inhibited by the inclusion of only one 'deemed to satisfy' clause to meet the requirement to prevent passage of moisture from the ground. This called for 100 mm concrete on hardcore and although other forms of construction were not excluded, in theory, this was the only method acceptable to building control officers and it rendered timber floors uneconomic. In Scotland two other methods were accepted, the use of hot bitumen sprayed on the area and the use of a damp-proof membrane such as polythene with a protective cover of 50 mm of concrete. The latter method is most widely used in North America and Scandinavia and if installed in the UK in accordance with the detail shown (Fig. 2.3) has the approval the NHBC and the Department of the Environment as shown in approved document C–Site preparation and resistance to moisture. As an additional and perhaps unnecessary safeguard the NHBC requires that the joists be treated with a preservative. The underfloor area should have adequate cross-ventilation in the approximate ratio of 1/300 of the floor area.

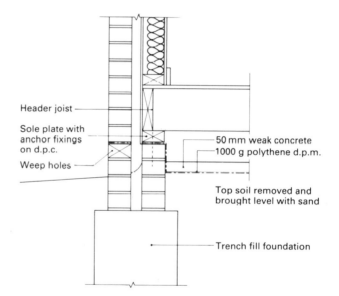

Fig. 2.3 Suspended timber ground floor

Timber floor construction

The construction of floors in timber frame is in many respects the same as in brick and block buildings but there are some important differences. Above the sole plate level all connections are timber to timber and no joists are supported on masonry. Each floor diaphragm runs through to the outside face of the studs in the exterior wall and is in place prior to the erection of the next set of wall and partition components (see Fig. 2.4). Where a suitably weatherproof floor sheathing such as plywood is specified, a safe working platform is provided at each floor level for each stage of erection. The functional requirements vary between ground, intermediate and compartment floors primarily in respect to fire resistance and sound transmission, the live load-bearing factor being a constant at 1.5 kN/m². Although it is not a requirement of the 1985 Building Regulations, designers are recommended to increase this design load to 2.0 kN/m² for intermediate or compart-

Fig. 2.4 Plywood floor sheathing being laid

ment floors supporting living rooms in order to reduce reverberation caused by the occasional party.

Intermediate floors in two-storey houses require a modified half-hour resistance and in three-storey houses a full half-hour resistance and methods of meeting these requirements are covered in Chapter 3 on dry lining. There are no requirements for acoustic insulation except in the case of compartment floors. The specific requirements for compartment floors are also covered in Chapter 3.

Joist selection

Almost all house plans utilize joists over a variety of spans and it is a common practice to allow the longest span to dictate the size, grade and spacing of the joists which is wasteful in terms of timber usage. There are several economic methods of accommodating different span requirements while maintaining a constant depth in the floor zone. The thickness or grade of joists may be varied although this can lead to problems in material

supply and site supervision. A more simple solution is to use the same joists throughout but to vary the spacing, closer together for the longer spans and further apart for the shorter ones (see Fig. 2.5). In adopting this method it should be noted that the thickness of the floor sheathing and the ceiling linings will be governed by the widest spacing. It should also be noted that the joists must be spaced to accept the dimension of the floor sheathing and ceiling linings. Since these panels are usually 2.4 m long and the end joints are staggered, the centre line of a joist should occur every 1.2 m. Consequently the modular spacing of the joists should be 300, 400, or 600 mm on centres and the in-line method of installation should be used rather than the overlap (see Fig. 2.6).

Another approach to the design of the floor structure which is particularly applicable to larger houses is to use beams to reduce the span of the floor joists. This can be effective not only in achieving economies in timber usage but also in adding another element of visual interest. In order to equalize any shrinkage which may

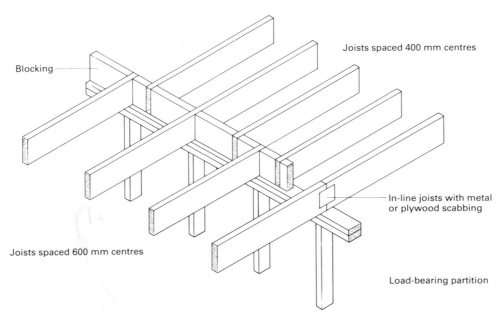

Blocking

Joists spaced 400 mm centres

Joists spaced 600 mm centres

In-line joists with metal or plywood scabbing

Load-bearing partition

Fig. 2.5 Variable joist spacing

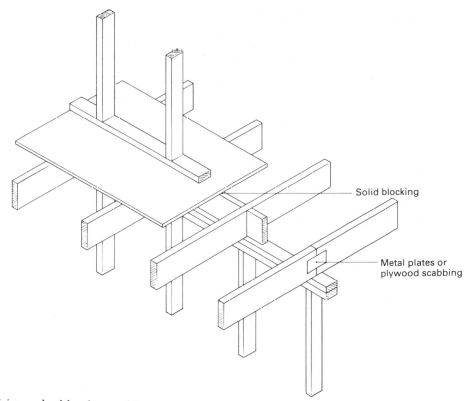

Solid blocking

Metal plates or
plywood scabbing

Fig. 2.6   In-line joists on load-bearing partition

occur in the floor zone it is essential that floor beams are installed at close to their equilibrium moisture content. This can be very difficult to achieve with large sections of timber but is standard practice in the manufacture of glue-laminated beams which are recommended for this particular use.

Should a clear ceiling line be required, the beam or flitch lintel can be designed to be the same depth as the floor joists and built in within the same vertical zone as the joists. Those at right angles either side of the beam can be supported on joist hangers.

Timber frame walls and partitions

The use of timber-framed load-bearing walls and partitions is the most essential difference between timber and brick and block construction. As with other elements in timber frame they are subject to design by a qualified structural engineer. Load-bearing walls are designed to transmit all of the vertical live and dead loads safely through to the foundations and to resist racking and overturning loads which result from wind pressure and in some instances from seismic shock or ground settlement. In conjunction with the application of internal linings, insulation and external claddings they must be structurally sound, weatherproof and durable with the thermal, acoustic and fire-resistant properties required by the Building Regulations. Non-load-bearing walls and partitions vary in their requirements depending on their locations but may incorporate several of the functions listed above.

Timber-framed walls consist of uniformly spaced vertical members called studs to which are nailed top and bottom rails usually of the same dimension. In load-bearing partitions openings for windows and doors are formed with timber lintels which are supported on shorter length studs called cripple studs which are

nailed to adjacent full length studs. There may be one or more cripple studs depending upon the load carried by the lintel. To provide dimensional stability during transport and erection, external panels are braced usually by the use of a sheet material such as an exterior quality plywood sheathing. By attaching the sheathing the external wall frames become rigid diaphragms, an essential element in providing the racking resistance of the building. Internal partitions are not usually braced but if required for structural reasons they may have sheathing applied and act as internal diaphragms to increase the racking resistance of the structure. Party walls in terraced housing are usually braced by diagonal timber members nailed to the frames and located in the cavity between the frames. Where required to provide fixings for wall-hung cabinets, plumbing fixtures, services, etc. horizontal members called noggings are nailed in between the studs. These are usually the same dimension as the studs with the face set vertically to provide a wider nailing surface and to facilitate the installation of services and the insulation in external walls.

For accurate construction studs should be specified as planed all round to precise dimensions at 19 per cent moisture content and the most commonly used size to date has been the Canadian CLS dimension 38 × 89 mm (nom. 2 × 4 in). This is virtually the minimum thickness on which to make a plasterboard joint with a width sufficient to accommodate services and an adequate amount of insulation. The width may be increased in the future if the standards of thermal insulation are improved. As a rule the studs are not highly stressed and the engineer is likely to specify a grade equivalent to Strength Class 3, e.g. GS to BS 4978 or NLGA No. 2 Structural Light Framing. It should be noted that NHBC requires all external wall-framing members to be treated with a preservative and BS 5268 has similar recommendations. To avoid the need to differentiate between timber members used in external and internal wall framing it is common practice for manufacturers to treat all wall framing with preservative.

Wall frame construction

The interior lining and the exterior sheathing materials are usually supplied in the metric modular size of 1.2 × 2.4 m. The standard spacing of the studs at 600, 400 or 300 mm centres is adopted to ensure that the joints in these materials will always occur on the centre line of a stud. Whichever spacing is adopted, it should be maintained throughout the length of the component. As Fig. 2.7 indicates, where a window opening does not occur on a module the spacing is maintained below the window sill. It also shows that where the length of the wall is not a multiple of the module only one stud spacing is required to be non-modular. Where the modular grid line is on the outside face of the stud the last stud spacing is reduced by the width of the adjoining component to allow the external sheathing to overlap and provide an additional connection between the components.

Additional supporting members are required at all corners and intersections to provide for adequate nailing together of the components and to provide backing for the sheathing and internal linings. In external walls this is best achieved by installing an additional stud as shown in Fig. 2.8, allowing space for the insulation to fit tightly into the corner. At corners in internal par-

titions it is usually more convenient to install the additional stud as shown in Fig. 2.9. At intersections between partitions, support may be provided by installing horizontal noggings at 600 mm centres (Fig. 2.10) The wall sheathing is fixed to the exterior wall frames after they have been squared up by checking the diagonal dimensions. It is standard practice in the UK to apply the sheathing with the long edges vertical, with all edges supported and fixed in accordance with the nailing schedule. An expansion gap of 2 mm should be left between the edges to allow for expansion if the plywood should pick up excess moisture during the construction process. In North America the sheathing is fixed with the long edge horizontal, either blocked or unblocked in accordance with engineering design.

Wall panels may be assembled with a single top rail or alternatively a top plate may be incorporated as a binder, and the designer must make the decision whether or not to use it. The top plate which must be used in small-panel construction combines a number of functions. It is usually the same dimension as the top rail and the two members together act as a beam between studs and allows joists and rafters to be located without reference to stud positions. Joints in the top rail and top plate must be made on the centre line of a stud and should not coincide. As shown in Fig. 2.7, the overlapping joints at corners and intersections bind the heads of components together and provide a positive location for partitions. Top plates should be selected in

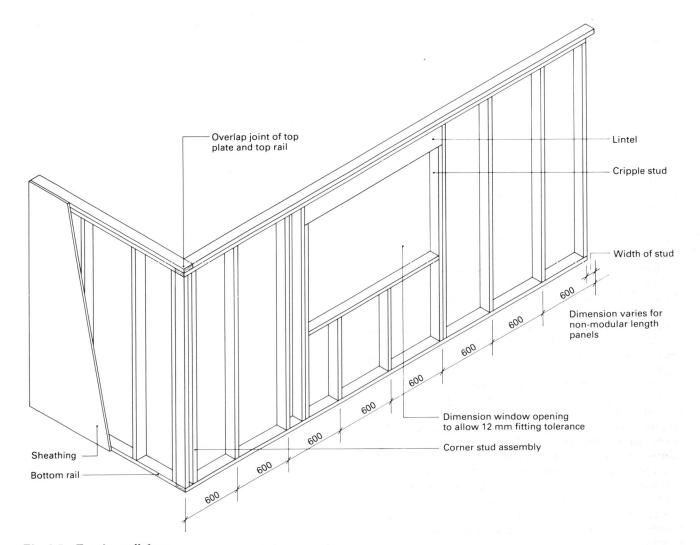

Fig. 2.7 Exterior wall frame

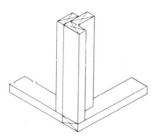

Fig. 2.8   Corner stud assemblies

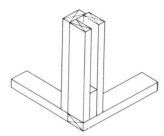

Fig. 2.9   Alternative corner stud assemblies

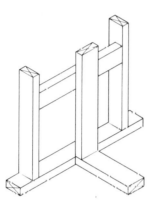

Fig. 2.10   Partition intersections

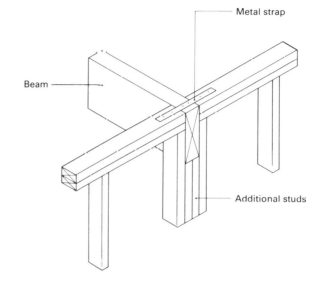

Fig. 2.11   Beam support

long lengths for straightness as an aid in aligning components. For convenience in fabrication and erection, non-load-bearing and load-bearing partitions are usually the same height and the top plates where specified are used on both. Where the top plates are not specified all joists and roof trusses must be aligned within 40 mm of the centre line of studs which requires considerable care in design and construction. In addition, 30 mm wide metal straps should be nailed to the top rail to connect components at joints and intersections. Where point loads from beams or purlins occur, they must be supported on additional studs (see Fig. 2.11) or a post. Where point loads occur on upper floors care must be taken to ensure that the load is fully supported down to the foundations.

Components are usually manufactured to a standard nominal height of 2.4 m and although gable end walls and sloping walls may be framed up by varying stud lengths they are usually framed up as separate components. All components should be manufactured with a minus tolerance of 3 mm in length to avoid any creep as a series of components are joined together.

Unless there are unusual design considerations all joints in timber-framed walls are made with nails in accordance with the schedule shown in Chapter 7, which shows the gauge, number and length for each location.

Openings in external walls

Windows and doors may be factory or site fixed and careful attention to detail is necessary to ensure that there is no possibility of rain penetration or air movement around the opening. Also since the window and door frames are supported by the timber frame, allowance must be made for differential movement between timber and masonry where it is used as the external cladding material. Straight-through joints which rely on mastic to seal any gaps should be avoided and one or other of the details illustrated should be used. Figure 2.12 shows a jamb detail with a planed 50 × 50 mm cavity stop which also acts as a weather-bar. The jamb and head details shown in Figs 2.13 and 2.14 incorporate a plywood or metal weather-bar let into the frame which provides a positive barrier and also a convenient method for fixing the joinery to the wall frame permitting the use of factory-finished window and door frames. The weather-bar is also used under the sill as Fig. 2.15 shows and incorporates a mastic sealant to accommodate differential movement. The required tolerances for differential movement are covered in Chapter 4 – Exterior finishes.

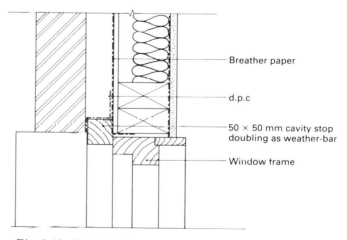

Fig. 2.12   Jamb detail

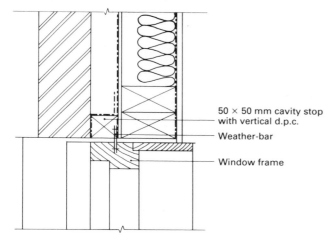

Fig. 2.13   Alternative jamb detail

50 × 50 mm cavity stop with vertical d.p.c.
Weather-bar
Window frame

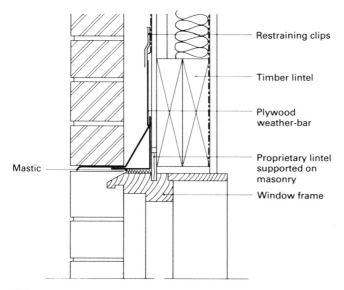

Restraining clips

Timber lintel

Plywood weather-bar

Proprietary lintel supported on masonry

Window frame

Mastic

Fig. 2.14   Window head detail

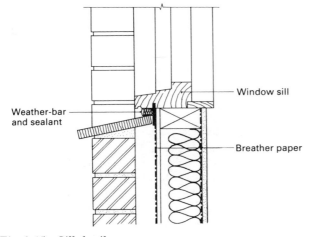

Window sill

Weather-bar and sealant

Breather paper

Fig. 2.15   Sill detail

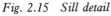

Upper-floor construction

The floor is usually constructed on the site though in some projects using crane erection large prefabricated panels are used. To maintain accuracy a minimum specification should call for joists to be regularized in width and thickness by planing one side and one edge. As Fig. 2.16 illustrates, where joists are at right angles to an exterior wall a continuous header joist is installed. This header joist helps to locate and stabilize the ends of the joists, acts as a cavity barrier for the floor cavity and provides a continuous nailing strip for the floor sheathing and the bottom rail of the wall framing. It is nailed to the ends of the joists and is skew-nailed to the plate as are the joists. Apart from the use of the header joist, timber floors are framed up in the traditional fashion and bear on timber plates set at a uniform height. Openings are formed by the use of headers and trimmers as indicated in Fig. 2.18 and while the design is the responsibility of the structural engineer the following guidelines are given as an aid to the draughtsmen.

1   Trimmers and headers should be doubled when their span exceeds 1.2 m.

2   Headers more than 1.8 m long should be supported on joist hangers.

3   Tail joists over 2.4 m long should be supported on joist hangers.

Headers and trimmers can be made by using double or triple joists thus reducing the requirement for different sizes or grades of timber in the specification. Laminated joists should be spiked together with two rows of nails at 300 mm centres.

Bridging of floor joists

Cross-bridging or herring-bone strutting is a traditional element in timber floor construction, its principal function being to distribute concentrated loads between a number of joists and to provide transverse stiffness. Research in North America and Scandinavia has shown that it is not effective in performing these functions which are performed quite satisfactorily by the floor sheathing. However, both BS 5268 : Part 2 and the NHBC Practice Note No. 5 require either herring-bone or solid strutting one row in spans from 2.5 to 4.5 m and two rows in spans over 4.5 m. NHBC further requires that solid strutting is a minimum thickness of 38 mm and at least three-quarters of the depth of the joists. The strutting may not fulfil its original function but its correct installation is important for other reasons. As emphasized previously, the accurate modular spacing of joists is essential to provide for the jointing of floor and ceiling linings. The strutting maintains this accuracy and prevents any twisting or misalignment of joists after installation. Additionally both British Gypsum and, when published, the Code of Practice for dry lining require that all the edges of gypsum board ceiling linings are supported. As indicated in Fig. 2.19, solid strutting can perform a dual function and should be located to coincide with the width of gypsum board specified. Where used primarily as a backing for the joints in the gypsum board or outside the jurisdiction of the NHBC it may be a nominal size of 50 × 75 mm. It must be accurately cut to length and preferably not installed until the floor sheathing is fixed.

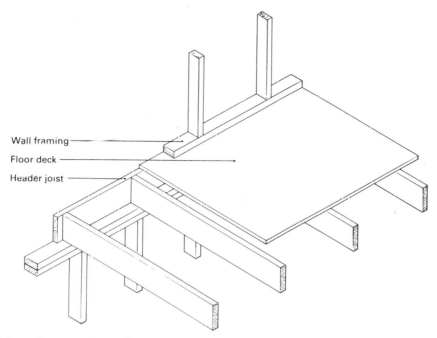

Wall framing

Floor deck

Header joist

Fig. 2.16 Joists at right angles to exterior wall

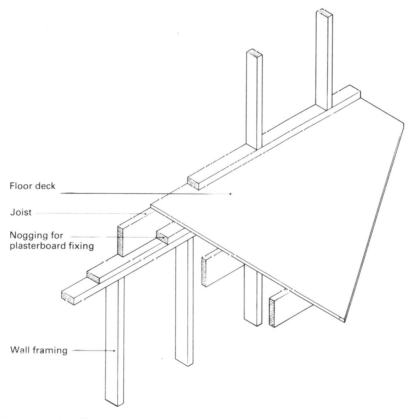

Floor deck

Joist

Nogging for
plasterboard fixing

Wall framing

Fig. 2.17 Joists parallel to external wall

Support of partitions

Partitions impose an additional load on the floor structure and special consideration must be given to their
support. As with other aspects of the structural design
this is the responsibility of the engineer. The following
information is intended primarily to assist the designer
in locating and supporting the partitions without having
to resort to the excessive use of structural timber.

Load-bearing partitions

In ground-floor construction load-bearing partitions are
usually supported directly from a suitably reinforced
slab or are located over sleeper walls. With modern clear
span roof structures where the roof loads are carried on
external walls they occur infrequently in the upper floor
of two-storey buildings but they are an integral part of
the intermediate floors of three-storey buildings. It is

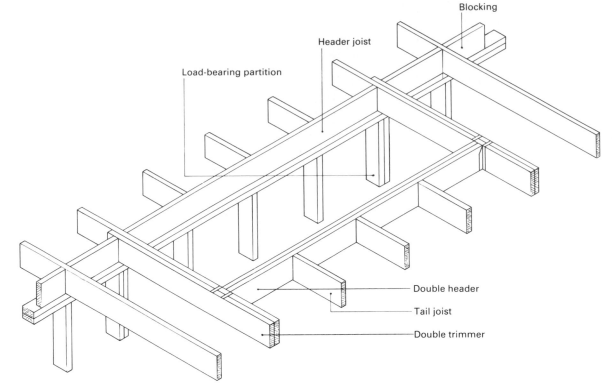

Fig. 2.18 Framing of floor opening

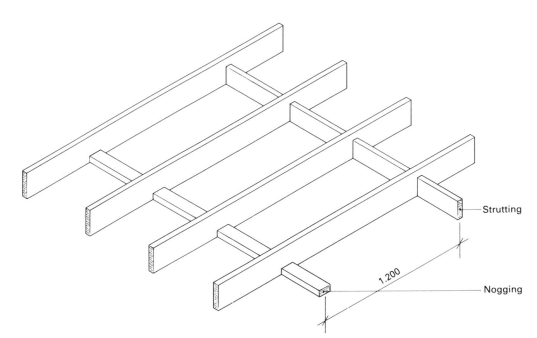

Fig. 2.19 Strutting and nogging of joists

common practice to locate load-bearing partitions directly over similar partitions in the floor below thus ensuring that the loads are carried directly to the foundations. Since this practice, if rigidly adhered to, would place unnecessary restrictions on the freedom of the plan layout, there are a number of options open to the designer. Load-bearing partitions running parallel to the joists may be carried on beams projecting into the room below or in the case of partitions without door openings the beams may be concealed within the thickness of the partition. Figure 2.20 shows a specially designed beam with timber flanges and plywood webs installed within a partition above the floor joists. Special attention

should be paid to the support of the ends of any beams to ensure that the loads are properly transferred to the foundations. Load-bearing partitions running at right angles to the joists should be located within one-quarter of the span from the bearing of the joists. Where lightweight external claddings are used joists may also be cantilevered over the external supporting wall. Depending upon the load carried at the end of the joists, the cantilever could be up to one-quarter of the span without any increase in joist size, subject to engineering calculations (see Figs 2.21 and 2.22). The designer should note that similar cantilevers can be employed internally.

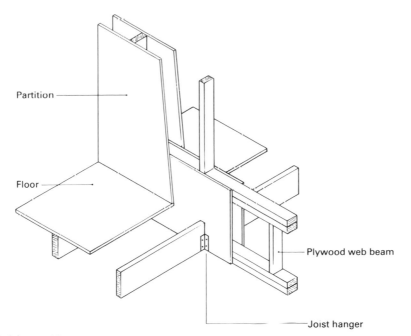

Fig. 2.20   Beam concealed in partition

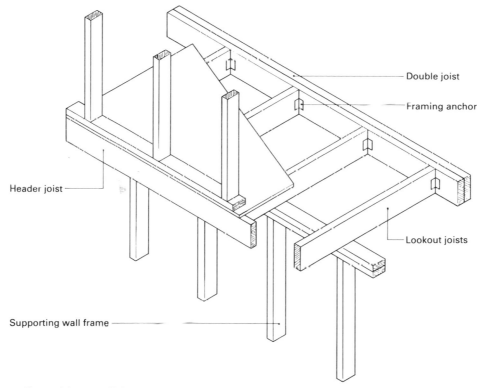

Fig. 2.21   Floor cantilever, joists parallel to wall

Non-load-bearing partitions

As a general rule non-load-bearing partitions may be placed in any location but the additional dead load placed on the floor structure requires the consideration of the designer. Where the partition runs parallel to the joists and is not located above a joist it should be supported on noggings at 600 mm centres. Depending upon the span of the joists relative to their maximum designed span, an additional joist may be required and in such cases a minimum space of 50 mm should be left between joists to facilitate the installation of services running from the floor into the partition.

Non-load-bearing partitions running at right angles to the joists can in most instances be supported without any increase in the floor structure except when the partition is located in the centre half of the span and the joists are spanning close to their design maximum.

Partitions are supported by and firmly fixed to the floor structure. When they have been plumbed vertical they are nailed at the head to the floor or roof construc-

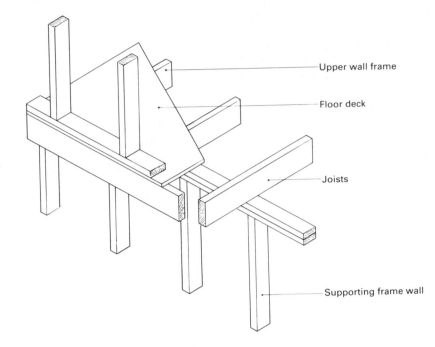

Upper wall frame

Floor deck

Joists

Supporting frame wall

Fig. 2.22   Floor cantilever, joists at right angles to wall

Noggings 600 mm centres

Fig. 2.23   Fixing of non-load-bearing partition to floor framing

tion. Where the partition is running parallel the overhead members noggings should be installed at 600 mm centres (see Fig. 2.23).

Floor decking

The materials most commonly used for the floor sheathing are T & G plywood, chipboard and softwood flooring and the choice made by the designer will have an effect on the construction programme. Exterior grade plywood which is installed as soon as the joists are fixed in position is virtually impervious to the effects of adverse weather conditions. It provides rigidity to the structure during the erection process and a safe working platform. Moisture-proof chipboard provides only temporary protection against the weather and should not be installed before the building is weathertight. Softwood floorboards should be kiln dried to their equilibrium moisture content in service of 12 per cent and also installed after the building is weathertight. Unlike plywood and chipboard it is unlikely to provide suitable substrate for thermoplastic tiles without an overlay of hardboard.

Plywood floor sheathing

Plywood should be specified as an exterior grade with a fully waterproof glue-line T & G on the long edges. It should be an unsanded grade equivalent to the Canadian COFI select sheathing or the American APA CC plugged and touch sanded or Sturdi-Floor. Plywood is installed with the long edges at right angles to the joists with the ends supported on the centre line of the joists. The end joints should be staggered with a 2 mm gap left to accommodate any expansion which could occur if the plywood were to be saturated during construction. The T & G joint on the long edges eliminates the need for installing noggings to prevent differential deflection between panels and is so profiled as to provide a gap to allow for expansion. The plywood provides a rigid horizontal diaphragm and should not be fully nailed until the section of building under construction has been aligned and plumbed. The use of ring-shank nails is recommended for fixing the plywood to the joists because their shorter length as compared to round wire nails reduces the possibility of nail popping as the joists dry to their equilibrium moisture content. Plywood does not provide a suitable surface for polyurethane or varnish but with a light sanding subsequent to the application of dry lining, plywood will provide a suitable substrate for any finish flooring.

Chipboard

Chipboard floor sheathing should be either Type II or Type II/III in accordance with BS 5669, 18 mm thickness for joist spacing up to 450 mm centres and 22 mm thickness for spacing up to 600 mm. Square-edged boards should be laid with the long edges parallel to the joists and with the edges supported on the centre line of the joists, the ends being supported by noggings. Tongued and grooved chipboard is installed with the long edges at right angles to the joists and with the ends falling on the centre line of the joists. In both cases suitable support is required around the perimeter of the boards (see Fig. 2.24). End joints should be staggered and an expansion gap of 2 mm per metre run of floor (min. 10 mm) allowed between the chipboard and any perimeter wall. As with plywood, ring-shanked nails should be used at a minimum of 9 mm from the edge of the board. Chipboard should 'condition' on site for at least 24 hours before being fixed. Detailed information is available from the Chipboard Promotion Association.

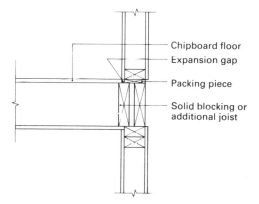

Fig. 2.24   Chipboard floor at external wall

Insulation

Currently there are no requirements for thermal insulation of ground floors except where fully exposed to the exterior. Heat loss through an uninsulated floor can be as high as 25 per cent of the total and whether concrete or timber the installation of insulation is both simple and cost effective. With concrete slabs perimeter insulation using expanded polystyrene either vertically to approximately 600 mm below grade or horizontally in a 1200 mm strip around the perimeter is the most economic. With a suspended timber floor over a partially vented space the whole area should be insulated using either expanded polystyrene supported on clips or battens or alternatively insulation batts supported on wire or nylon mesh.

Roof construction

Essentially the roof structure of a timber frame house will be the same as for a brick and block building and must satisfy the same requirements in terms of structural stability, durability and weathertightness. Over the past twenty years it has become standard practice to use factory-fabricated trusses at 600 mm centres and this type of roof does provide economies in terms of a reduction in material content and the use of site labour. These economies have been achieved with the loss of usable attic storage space and the possibility of developing the roof space into habitable accommodation that is associated with earlier forms of roof construction. As houses have tended to become smaller over the years the use of 'W' trusses could be considered in many instances to be a false economy, and as the following diagrams indicate there are alternative constructions which for little additional cost could provide storage space, additional accommodation or the opportunity to expand living accommodation in the future.

Attic storage truss

A clear span factory-fabricated trussed rafter designed for installation at 600 mm centres to provide clearly defined and accessible storage space where the height is not sufficient to provide habitable accommodation. The vertical struts may be lined or partially lined to provide lateral stability (see Fig. 2.5).

Attic truss

A clear span factory-fabricated trussed rafter designed to be installed at 600 mm centres to provide habitable accommodation in the roof space (see Fig. 2.26). The ridge component is not part of the structural truss and is usually supplied separately to reduce the height during transport. The timber members are approximately twice the size of those in a 'W' truss and depending upon the span and pitch may require the use of a crane for installation. In accordance with engineering design the spacings may be varied to accommodate dormer windows, roof lights and stairs. The designer should note that stairs should run parallel to the trusses.

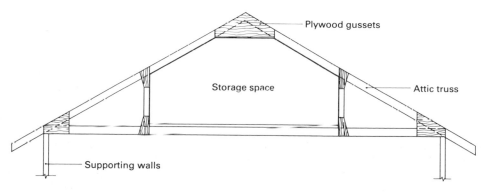

Fig. 2.25   Attic storage truss

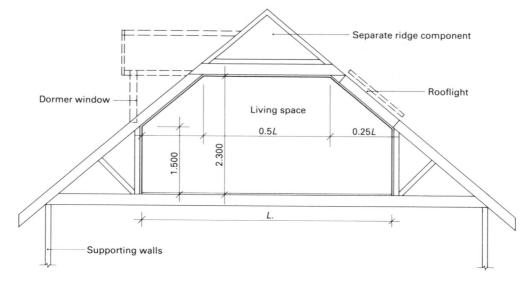

Fig. 2.26   Attic truss

Mansard truss

A clear span, site-fabricated truss with the joints formed by plywood gussets nailed to each side of the timber members providing almost total utilization of the roof space. The floor is not an integral part of the truss and is designed to be supported conventionally on load-bearing walls. Windows may be installed in the plane of the roof or inset as indicated in the diagram. As an indication of the size of members, 44 × 195 mm timbers should span approximately 10 m spaced at 600 mm centres. Wind bracing is provided by plywood sheathing applied to the steeper pitches.

Stressed skin panels

A stressed skin panel consists of a framework of timber members with a sheet material such as plywood rigidly attached to one or both faces by nailing and/or gluing. The attachment of the plywood adds very considerably to the structural performance of the joists and provides a very useful floor or roof component for spans up to 6 m. As a roof component the panels can span from wall to wall or from purlin to purlin as shown in Fig. 2.28. The purlins shown are indicated as plywood web beams which in this instance can also be used to support the

floor joists. As with the other structural systems illustrated useful unobstructed attic space is provided.

'W' trusses

British standard 5268 : Part 3 covers the structural design of 'W' trusses and this is usually the prerogative of the manufacturers of the punched metal plates which are most commonly used for the joints between members. Bracing of trussed rafters is required in the plane of the rafters and also the ceiling and provision must be made for supporting the water storage tank. As with other structural members, the spacing must be consistently accurate with the module usually at 600 mm centres. Initially this accuracy can be achieved by using continuous runners on top of the ceiling chords at the node points and subsequently by installing noggings to support the edges of the ceiling lining. Additional noggings are installed between the trusses at 600 mm centres to support the heads of partitions which run parallel to the trusses. The trusses are usually fixed to the top plate by skew-nailing from either side, care being taken not to damage the metal plates. In areas of high winds proprietary truss clips are used to provide a more positive attachment.

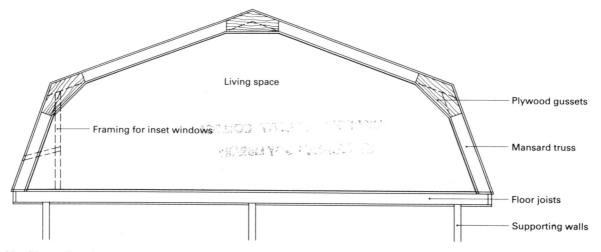

Fig. 2.27   Mansard roof truss

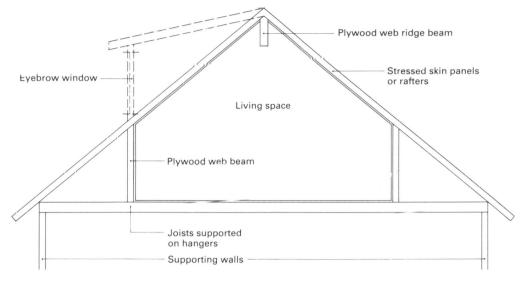

Fig. 2.28   Purlin beams

Plywood gussets

It is worth noting that BS 5268 : Part 3 permits the use of nailed or glued plywood gussets in lieu of pressed metal plate connectors. Plywood gussets because of their much larger dimensions tend to produce a stiffer and stronger truss and where nailed gussets are specified allow the facility where required for site fabrication.

Durability and ventilation

With the exception of the use of roof timbers in certain areas in southern England infested by longhorn beetle and joists in flat roof construction there is no mandatory requirement for preservative treatment. The performance and durability of the roof structure are largely dependent upon ensuring that leakage or condensation in the roof space does not cause the moisture content of any member to remain above 22 per cent which would cause fungal decay in untreated timber. If it is assumed that the roofing material and the flashings do not permit water penetration from the exterior then any potential problem is likely to be caused by the condensation of water vapour migrating into the roof space from the interior of the house. Traditionally the movement of vapour has been restricted by a vapour-proof membrane installed between the ceiling lining and the insulation but this is no longer an NHBC requirement. Whether or not a vapour barrier is specified, the accumulation of water vapour in roof spaces must be prevented by the provision of adequate ventilation and recommendations are given in BS 5250 : *The Control of Condensation in Dwellings* and also approved document F. These may be paraphrased as follows:

(a)   a 10 mm gap continuously along each side of a roof with a pitch over 15°;

(b)   a 25 mm gap continuously along each side of a roof with a pitch under 15°.

Provided that each area in the roof has adequate through ventilation alternative methods can be used to replace supplement strip ventilation. Ridge vents, gable end vents or individual eaves vents can all be used and the larger vents may have the advantage of facilitating the installation of insect screening. Where the roof covering is tiles or slates some adventitious dissipation of vapour will occur providing that the roofing felt is of a breather type in accordance with BS 2747. In cold flat roof construction, i.e. where the insulation is below the roofing membrane, a vapour barrier must be installed between the insulation and the ceiling lining and each joist cavity must be cross-ventilated. This same requirement applies to rooms in the roof where the insulation is located in the space between the rafters with the ceiling lining fixed to the rafters. Care should be taken to ensure that the installation of the insulation does not block the passage of ventilation.

Chapter 3
Installation of services

Accurate dimensions must be given on the drawings to locate service entry positions in the ground-floor slab. These positions should be shown on the sole plate drawing to ensure that no perforation of the slab coincides with a sole plate and wall cover. Preferably two dimensions should be given for each entry position, at right angles to each other from the edge of the slab to the centre of the service pipe or duct. In calculating these dimensions, allowance must be made for the thickness of plasterboard and possibly the thickness of the skirting on the wall over the sole plate, i.e. the service entries should not appear close up to the side of sole plates and should never penetrate them.

Where earthenware soil pipes are located through the slab, besides an allowance for plasterboard and skirting, before arriving at the position of the centre of the pipe it must be remembered that the pipe will have a collar above the slab and will in fact be approximately 150 mm in diameter for a 100 mm pipe.

Wastes from kitchen sinks and lavatory basins on or near external walls on ground floors, can go through the slab and connect up on the outside to a back-inlet gully. This avoids unsightly waste pipes penetrating external walls and running down the elevations to discharge over gully gratings.

Gas carcassing

Gas carcassing drawings for individual houses are seldom produced in the UK. For estate work, i.e. many houses of same or similar type, the Gas Boards will normally provide a schematic carcassing drawing. It is best for the designer to provide the Gas Board with layout plans to show the position of gas appliances and sole plate drawings on which they can mark their carcassing runs. For individual one-off houses, the designer must liaise with the workmen who arrive on site to carry out the work to ensure accurate positioning of outlets.

Ground-floor gas carcassing is usually carried out on top of the slab, after the fixing of sole plates and before laying of the screed (see Fig. 3.1). Again all upstands for connections in the horizontal runs must be sufficiently clear of the sole plates to avoid plasterboard and skirting above and also to permit the use of a spanner or wrench in making the connection to the appliance. If the gas carcassing pipe runs across a sole plate in any particular case, care must be taken to see that both cut ends of the transversed sole plate are adequately secured to the slab. On repetitive work on estates, gas carcassing can be prefabricated and so save time and expense. The prefabricated pipe runs can be put in place immediately after fixing of sole plates and before commencement of screed. The installers have an open area in which to work without the need for cutting holes through walls as is necessary with masonry construction.

Gas appliances needing a flue are best provided by the installation of an insulated metal flue such as Twin-wall insulated chimney by Selkirk. These can be housed in ducts when running up through the house and perforate the roof space and roof covering in exactly the same way as the SVP (Soil and Vent Pipe).

Gas boilers, if located on external walls, are easily served by balanced flues. They must not, however, be located near windows nor in internal angles.

Incoming electrical services

Electric services normally enter a house via an externally mounted meter box supplied by the Electricity Board. This is either surface mounted direct on to the cladding or recessed into brick cladding. Where the former

Fig. 3.1 Service and drain connections accurately set in slab

method is used, the supply cable rises from the ground and enters through the bottom of the meter box. Where the latter method is used, the supply cable can rise in the cavity behind the brickwork and up into the meter box. The meter box should always be located in an accessible position to enable the meters to be read with no inconvenience to the occupier or meter reader. Close consultation must be maintained with the Electricity Supply Authority and agreement reached in respect of entry positions and positions of meter boxes.

Plumber and heating engineer

Detailed drawings are seldom produced showing accurate positions of pipe runs. The designer determines on his drawings where he requires the sanitary fittings, boiler, flue, radiators etc. The plumber and heating engineer will sometimes provide diagrammatic drawings showing how all these are connected and made to work but if possible he should be made to produce drawings showing the intended pipe runs. It is helpful if these are superimposed on the designer's drawings – plans, joist layouts and roof truss layouts. This enables the designer to check that the adequacy of the timber frame is not being impaired by runs of pipework needing holes and notching in the wrong places. If the plumber and heating engineer is not experienced in timber frame construction, he should be made aware of the points made in the remainder of this section at the time of tender.

The accuracy of site dimensions obtained with timber frame construction, when components are made off site in factory conditions, should soon convince the plumber and heating engineer (normally the same tradesman when a wet system of heating is employed), that he can safely prefabricate his main pipe runs. If prefabricated, pipes that run through the floor zone can be dropped into notches in the top of the joists during construction, i.e. immediately before laying the floor deck. Plumbers and heating engineers find this much easier than working on the underside of joists after the shell is completed. In order not to delay the shell erection, however, it is imperative that the pipe runs are prefabricated and ready for fixing at the correct time. The installer of the pipes must work as a member of the shell erection team. If pipe runs are notched on top of the joists, it is strongly recommended that the location of the runs be pencilled on top of the floor deck to prevent nails from puncturing the pipes during the fixing of the deck material. Similarly, if the pipe runs are notched on the underside of the joists, the plasterboard ceiling boards should be so marked for the same reason. A little care and attention in this direction could avoid no end of troubles later.

Too much care cannot be exercised in notching joists. It must be remembered that the whole timber shell has been engineered and calculations produced to prove its adequacy. Notching cannot, therefore, be carried out at random but only in accordance with the precise limits set by the designer or engineer.

Clause B6 in approved document A requires that notches and holes in simply supported joists should be within the following limits:

Notches not more than $\frac{1}{8}$ the joist depth located in the first quarter of the $\frac{3}{8}$ span not closer to the support than 0.07 of the span.

Holes drilled should be no more than $\frac{1}{4}$ the depth of the joist, located in the neural zone, at least three diameters apart centre to centre, and between 0.25 and 0.4 times the span from the support.

No holes or notches should be permitted in prefabricated trusses.

A piece of felt or sacking between hot-water pipes and floor joists where they cross will assist in preventing those annoying noises that can occur as pipes within a dwelling begin to get hot and expand, and again when they cool off and shrink.

Hot- and cold-water pipes in the floor zone can sometimes be threaded through the joists from the outside of the structure by drilling holes in a straight line through the neutral zone (mid depth), see Fig. 3.2. No prefabrication can be incorporated by this method as only straight runs can be threaded through. Angled joints have to be made while the threaded pipe is in position within the floor. This method keeps the pipes away from flooring and ceiling nails but does entail working between the joists and under the floor deck to make connections which can sometimes be awkward and always presents a fire risk when a blowlamp has to be used in a confined space surrounded by timber.

Fig. 3.2 Heating pipes threaded through neutral axis of floor joists

The largest single problem encountered on handovers is that caused by water leaks and they can be very costly to cure in time, money and inconvenience to the occupier – taking down ceilings, drying out the structure, furniture, carpets, etc.; repairing the leak; renewing ceilings and redecorating. Sometimes a nail driven into a pipe will not show a leak for some time, especially with an annular-ringed shank nail. Until the pipe gets hot and expands, the nail will sometimes seal the hole sufficiently to conceal the leak for a considerable time before it becomes apparent on the surface.

Where cold-water pipes are run in close proximity to hot-water pipes in the floor zone, the latter should be lagged to prevent the cold water from becoming warm, to prevent heat loss and to minimize the risk of surface condensation on the cold-water pipes. In the roof space, all water pipes should be individually lagged and the overflow pipes should drop vertically from the water storage and expansion tanks and fall to the outside within the depth of the ceiling joist, to which they can be clipped. If the overflow pipes run straight from the tanks to the discharge point, they form an additional hazard in the limited amount of manoeuvring area within the roof space formed by prefabricated roof trusses and tend to sag considerably because of the inability to provide adequate clipping across the struts of the roof trusses. Another point to remember is that if showers are to be provided on the top floor of the house, it is advantageous to place the cold-water storage tank as high as possible within the roof space, thus giving a larger head of water and, therefore, more pressure at the shower outlet.

Timber floor joists in all forms of construction shrink in their depth after installation and further drying out. This is evidenced in a traditionally built house, soon after occupation, by a gap appearing between the top of the bath and the underside of the wall tiling around the top of the bath. This does not happen in a timber platform frame house because the internal partitions and inner leaf of external walls all sit on the floor deck so that, as the joists shrink, bath and walls go down together. Nevertheless, it is important to see that the joint between the top of the bath and the underside of the tiles is well waterproofed with one of the proprietary brands of silicone sealing compounds available for the purpose, to avoid possible ingress of water into the timber structural frame.

Before leaving the plumber and heating engineer, it is important to mention an often disregarded point of construction. Bearers at right angles to the joists and spanning over at least two joists must be placed under each leg of the bath and, if the hot-water cylinder stands on the floor deck, it too should rest on two bearers at right angles to the joists and spanning over at least two. If the legs of a bath are allowed to rest directly on the floor deck, they could occur midway between floor joists, causing considerable deflection in the floor deck and a consequential breakdown of the seal between the top of the bath and the underside of the wall tiling.

There are plumbing and heating installations, generally only in one-off houses, where the installers have gone to great lengths to conceal all water pipes and, sometimes, even waste pipes. Apart from it being contrary to most, if not all, water regulations and good building practice, the resultant notching of studs to accommodate horizontal runs can have serious effects on the sufficiency of the structural design, cause additional hazards for leaks when nailing plasterboard and create great upheaval in locating and repairing leaks occurring after a house is occupied.

Most manufacturers of plastic waste pipes, rainwater pipes and SVPs print their name, BS number, etc. in a contrasting colour in one continuous line along the length of each piece of pipe produced. When fixing these pipes, it is quite easy to ensure that the line of printing is turned towards the surface to which it is being fixed and thus become hidden from view. This is a small point to consider but it is surprising how often black rainwater pipes can be seen with white lettering running down their full length and white waste pipes from lavatory basins in bathrooms running to a duct with red lettering fully visible.

Electrician

Drawings showing the electrical installation normally only show the positions of switches, lighting points, socket outlets, meters, etc. Apart from showing diagrammatically which switch controls which lighting point, no attempt is made by the designer to show where the wiring runs. It is therefore imperative that the electrician has full information, at the time he prepares his price, of where he can, and where he cannot, run his wiring and the particular requirements of timber frame construction as set out in the remainder of this section.

When determining the position of switches and socket outlets it is worth remembering that those located on external and load-bearing walls will need to be fire stopped (see Fig. 3.4), while those on non-load-bearing walls need no such protection. Time and money can therefore be saved by locating as many as possible on non-load-bearing walls where this can be done without impairing their use. Similarly, placing switches and socket outlets back to back on a wall between two areas is also economical.

Generally speaking, the electrician finds the wiring of a timber frame house easier than the wiring of its traditional masonry built counterpart. Apart from working in warm and dry conditions, drilling holes in timber and fixing switch boxes and socket outlets to timber noggings is much easier than drilling holes in, and fixing fittings to, masonry.

When wiring is run in the floor zone at right angles to the joists, it should be run through holes drilled in the neutral axis of the joists. The size and positions of the holes should be in accordance with the limits set by the designer and clause Se 7 of the NHBC Handbook. Where the wiring runs parallel to the joists, it should be adequately stapled to the sides of the joists well clear of the top and bottom edges, where it can be safe from any nailing of the floor deck and plasterboard ceiling (see Fig. 3.3). In the roof space, truss members should never be drilled and the stapling of the wiring to the sides of the trusses should be done with the same strict caution as for the floor joists. The wiring must be clear of the range of the ceiling plasterboard nails which can sometimes miss in fixing to the ceiling joist of the truss.

Fig. 3.3 Wiring clipped in safe position along sides of joists. Wiring drops not clipped to sides of studs

When wiring drops in walls from floor zone or roof space to socket outlets and switches, it should never be stapled to the sides of the studs. This enables rewiring to be carried out without removing wall plasterboard i.e. the space between two adjacent studs and the back of plasterboard and/or sheathing plywood, forms a convenient conduit. There is also less likelihood of a loosely hanging vertical cable being penetrated by a plasterboard nail that misses the stud.

Care must always be taken to ensure that all wiring is kept clear of hot-water pipe runs. Although this is a rule of good practice in all forms of construction, site operatives sometimes become over-enthusiastic when they experience the speed with which they can work with timber frame housing. Such enthusiasm is to be encouraged but has to be carefully monitored. An example is where the electrician finds he can thread his wiring through the same holes or notches that the plumber has used for his hot-water pipe.

The fire-stopping requirement for electrical outlets and switches in external and load-bearing walls is normally achieved by fixing 38 mm thick timber or two pieces of 12.7 mm plasterboard, or one piece of 19 mm, the full width and depth between studs, top and bottom of the nogging holding the electrical outlet box (see (Fig. 3.4).

Fig. 3.4 Wiring in external wall to socket outlets showing fire stopping using plasterboard off-cuts

Metal electrical boxes to receive switches and socket outlets in non-load-bearing walls can be fixed to the side of studs and thus save the cost of supplying and fixing a nogging. In the USA and Canada, such boxes are readily available and are fixed with two 99 mm galvanized or sherardized nails through projecting lugs on each side of the box, top and bottom. The face plate of the switch or socket outlet secured over the plasterboard ensures a firm fixing. Finally, electricians wiring a timber frame house, should always be persuaded to attend on themselves and not expect attendance by the main contractor. After all, they only need holes drilled in timber which is far easier and less time consuming than chasing in, or drilling through, blocks and bricks as required in masonry construction.

Insulation, condensation and vapour barrier

Before any covering-in of the inside of the components takes place, a check must be made, with the aid of a moisture meter, to see that the moisture content of the timber is 19 per cent or below. When timber is below 19 per cent moisture content, the possibility of fungal attack and decay is negligible. Studs at the sides of external openings and bottom rails of panels are most likely to have the highest moisture content and they,

therefore, should be the locations to check. If the correct timber is specified and supplied and if it has not been stored uncovered for an exceptionally long period in bad weather, the chances of a moisture content over 19 per cent are remote. Should it be in excess, given good weather with windows and doors left open by day, the moisture content will soon drop to the acceptable level.

Insulation

Thermal insulation requirements of the Building Regulations are easily achieved in timber frame construction by placing insulation materials in the wall and ceiling cavities of the timber frame. Choice of claddings does not significantly affect the thermal resistance of an external wall. Solid concrete ground floors should certainly be insulated around the perimeter of the slab and some designers are now specifying, instead of a sand and cement screed, 50 mm thick battens fixed to slab at 600 mm centres to receive plywood or chipboard flooring with 50 mm insulation (normally rigid polystyrene sheets) laid between the battens. With suspended timber floors, insulation can be placed between floor joists in the same manner as it is placed between studs in external walls but supported on a nylon net.

Paper-backed insulation quilt with selvedged edges (see Fig. 3.5), is made to suit stud centres commonly used in timber frame construction. The spaces between studs are covered with the insulation which is face-fixed by staples through the paper-backed selvedged edges into the face of the studs (see Fig. 3.6). Great care should be taken when cutting the insulation to suit the height of the timber panels to ensure that it is not cut

Fig. 3.5 Paper-backed Rocksil Timberfill insulating quilt (PF1). Note the projecting paper edges for stapling into face of studs

Fig. 3.6   Timberfill PF1 being stapled into position using a grip stapler

Fig. 3.7   Rocksil Insulation Quilt being laid in roof space

short, leaving a cold bridge at the top or bottom. It is far better for it to be cut a little too long than too short as the surplus can always be tucked in. If the fixers of the insulation are provided with a trestle table, standard full height lengths of insulation can be pre-cut more accurately than fixing straight from the roll and cutting off at the bottom with a knife. The insulation should always be on the warm side of the wall it is protecting, i.e. never push it back between the studs to rest on the inside face of the sheathing. The paper-backed insulation face-fixed to the edge of the studs ensures that it is kept in the correct location, normally 80 mm thick to fit cavity 89 mm deep.

Other forms of insulation placed between studs are available but the paper-backed insulation quilt is the most commonly used and the best for the purpose.

In extreme cases, very exposed sites or sites in exceptionally cold climates, very high thermal insulation may be required in the external walls. This can be achieved by using larger studs in the external framing – 38 × 140 mm (2 × 6 in) and so enable up to 140 mm thick insulation to be used. Because of the larger section stud, it may be possible to increase their centres but this will depend on the particular design, the structural calculations and the thickness of lining material.

Thermal insulation must also take into account external openings – windows and doors. Large single-glazed windows and draughty external door and window frames can minimize the effect of the high insulation value of timber frame walls. Draughtproofed windows and doors with double glazing should be a minimum standard. Triple glazing and insulated external doors are now becoming normal in Scandinavia and Canada.

Ceiling insulation in roof spaces is exactly as for masonry construction. It can be of varying thicknesses from 80 mm upwards and there is a variety of materials available, such as Rocksil or Fibreglass quilt which are rolled out between trusses as shown in Fig. 3.7, loose vermiculite spread between trusses and patent foams blown into position by mechanical means.

Thermal insulation is provided to prevent heat loss, thus conserving energy to provide the heat within the dwelling. The heat loss through building elements is measured by a U value in units of watts per square metre per degree Centigrade (W/m^2 °C) temperature difference from face to face of the element. The lower the U value, the lower the heat loss. The Building Regulations now require a minimum U value through external walls of all houses of 0.6 W/m^2 °C. A normal timber frame house with 80 mm insulation between studs, plywood sheathing and brick cladding will provide a U value of O.4 W/m^2 °C.

Condensation

Considerable quantities of water vapour are added to the indoor air by normal household activities such as cooking, laundering, bathing, paraffin heaters. etc. This produces an internal vapour pressure higher than that outdoors, with the result that high-pressure vapour builds up indoors and tends to flow to the lower pressure outdoors. If the vapour is allowed to flow through a well-insulated wall, it will condense on the colder regions within the wall. This is known as interstitial condensation.

When this vapour hits a cold solid masonry wall or a cold sheet of glass in a window, it immediately condenses on the surface. This is known as surface condensation. The well-insulated timber frame construction provides a warm inner surface and the vapour barrier is provided to prevent the water vapour from passing through the warm areas to reach the cold areas. Here, it would condense within the wall structure, causing the moisture content of the timber structure to rise after every effort has been made to ensure that it is below 19 per cent before being sealed in.

Considerable thought has been given to the problem of condensation and the problem has virtually been eliminated in timber frame housing design. It still remains important, however, for the occupants to realize that condensation will always occur where warm and moist internal air is in contact with cold inside surfaces, such as a single sheet of glass in a window. This often leads to water running down the glass, staining the window frame and causing mould growth. Occupiers of houses often refer to this as leaking windows. Ventilation is, at all times, a prerequisite of a condensation-free house and this must be realized by occupants despite the need for heat conservation.

Electrical extract fans discharging to the outside air and fitted to kitchens and bathrooms, greatly assist in combating condensation.

The Building Research Establishment (BRE) has published an information Paper on condensation, reference IP 1/81.

We have seen the importance of an impervious vapour barrier on the inside face of external timber frame wall units and the underside of roof trusses.

Vapour barrier

The vapour barrier which covers the internal face of the whole of the external walls, party walls and top-floor ceiling must be of an impervious sheet material, usually 250 gauge (0.06 mm) low-density polythene membrane to BS 3012 : 1970. It should be well lapped at all joints by at least 100 mm and adequately stapled to the face of studs and plates, and to the underside of the roof trusses. Great care must be taken to ensure a complete seal and, where openings have to be provided for switch boxes, etc. they must not be cut so large as to allow a leakage and discontinuity of the vapour barrier.

The vapour barrier is placed on the warm side of the insulated walls and top ceiling, directly behind the plasterboard linings, to minimize the passage of water vapour from the interior of the house into the structure. A moisture content in the timber of 19 per cent or less and the standard of thermal insulation are thus maintained.

Some designers have started to omit the vapour barrier from top-floor ceilings of dwellings with pitched roofs. The theory here is that the greatly improved ventilation of roof spaces now demanded by the Building Regulations will dissipate the moisture vapour when it penetrates through to the roof space. Indeed, some designers believe it is an ideal way of disposing of the vapour. No harm appears to have taken place when the top-floor ceiling barrier was used and it may therefore be a false economy to omit it now. The NHBC regulations do not require a top-floor ceiling vapour barrier.

Internal linings

As well as providing a base for decorative finishes and a strong surface capable of withstanding normal wear and tear, the internal linings to ceilings and walls may have to assist in providing fire resistance and prevention of sound transmission as required by the Building Regulations. Gypsum plasterboard is a material which can be used to meet all these criteria and which has been tested for fire resistance and flame spread as well as for its sound-absorbing qualities. Plasterboard has for many years been a familiar feature of the building scene and is the most natural choice of lining for timberframed elements. British Gypsum Limited, the makers of gypsum plasterboard in the UK, have developed variations of the standard product and the following types of board are among those now available, all manufactured in accordance with BS 1230 : Part 1: 1985.
Gypsum Plasterboard.

Gyproc wallboard

Gyproc wallboard (see Fig. 3.8), is used in dry construction work to provide wall and ceiling linings. The board has one decorative surface for direct decoration and is available with tapered and square edges according to joint treatment required. Tapered-edge boards provide a flat seamless surface equal to traditional plasterwork, after the correct joint treatment has been completed. Gyproc wallboard is fixed as a lining to timber frame walls and ceilings and is also available in an insulating grade.

Gyproc DUPLEX Plasterboards

This is Gyproc plasterboard with metallized polyester bonded to the back of the board. It has a water vapour resistance in excess of 15 MNs/g (Mega Newtons per second gram), the recommended minimum value for a vapour check material. Gyproc vapour-check wallboard is used to help prevent interstitial condensation but it will be realized that the joints will not be protected with a vapour check and great care must be exercised to see that the surface on the back is not damaged at all.

Gyproc Fireline board

Gyproc Fireline board is a gypsum plasterboard containing glassfibre and other additives in the core to improve its fire protection performance. The board is 12.5 mm thick with a decorative face and tapered or square edges. It can be used to provide improved fire protection to timber frame walls and ceilings.

Gyproc plank

This is 19 mm thick plasterboard available in 600 mm widths only. Square-edge plank has two grey surfaces and is generally used in timber frame construction behind the finishing layer of tapered-edge wallboard in order to achieve the required degree of fire resistance.

Gyproc moisture-resistant board

Gyproc moisture-resistant board has a gypsum core protected by a silicone additive and is lined on both sides with moisture-repellent liners. While being resistant to moisture, it is permeable to water vapour so allowing the structure to breathe. It can be used where there is exposure to external conditions during construction. It can be used for soffits to canopies, eaves, car ports and walkways and is recommended as a backing material in high moisture areas such as shower enclosures.

Gyproc thermal board and vapour-check thermal board

This board combines the qualities of Gyproc wallboard with the high thermal insulation of expanded polystyrene to form a versatile insulating lining board for walls and ceilings. However, while providing some insulation and a lining with one fixing, the thickness of the material means a loss of room area and the facility of fixing insulation between studs with no loss of room area is lost when this material is used on timber frame.

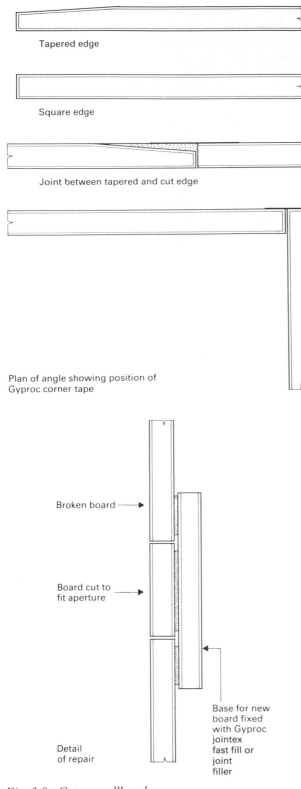

Fig. 3.8 Gyproc wallboard

TABLE OF DIMENSIONS

Width	Thickness	Length Tapered edge	Square edge
Gyproc wallboard			
600 mm	9.5 mm	1800 mm	1800 mm
	12.5 mm		1829 mm
		2286 mm	2286 mm
		2350 mm	2350 mm
		2400 mm	2400 mm
		2438 mm	2438 mm
		2700 mm	2700 mm
		3000 mm	3000 mm
900 mm	9.5 mm	As above	As above
	12.5 mm		
1200 mm	9.5 mm	As above; and	As above (except
	12.5 mm	3300 mm	1829 mm)
		3600 mm*	
Gyproc plank			
600 mm	19.0 mm	2350 mm	2350 mm
		2400 mm	2400 mm
		2700 mm	2700 mm
		3000 mm	3000 mm
		3200 mm	3200 mm

Fire protection

Plasterboard linings provide good fire protection owing to the unique behaviour of the gypsum core when subjected to high temperatures. As a result of their performance when tested to BS 476 : Parts 6 and 7, the surfaces of standard Gyprocwallboard, Gyproc Fireline board and plastic-faced plasterboards are designated Class 0 as defined in approved document B, appendix A, clause A8.

Tests

(a) BS 476 : 1981 : Part 6. *Method of Test for Fire Propogation For Products.* Index of performance (I) not exceeding 12 and a sub-index (i_1) not exceeding 6 (both sides).

(b) BS 476 : 1971 : Part 7. *Surface Spread of Flame Tests For Materials.* Class 1 (both sides).

	Thickness (mm)	*Thermal resistance $m^2 K/W$★*
Gyproc plasterboard	9.5	0.06 m^2
	12.5	K/W
	15.0	0.08
	19.0	0.12
Fireline board	12.7	0.05
Moisture-resistant board	9.5	0.05
	12.5	0.06
Duplex boards†	9.5	0.41
	12.5	0.43
Thermal board	25.0	0.42
	32.0	0.59
	40.0	0.81
	50.0	1.08
Urethane laminate	25.0	0.67
	32.0	0.99
	40.0	1.35

★ m^2 K/W = Metre^2/Kelvin (Centigrade) Watts
† Duplex boards have a reflective aluminium backing with a low emissivity surface which when facing a cavity gives enhanced thermal resistance values. The thermal resistance value quoted is for this surface facing an unventilated cavity not less than 25 mm wide.

Properties of plasterboard

Thickness (mm)	*Weight (kg/m^2)*
9.5	6.5–8.5
9.5 (moisture resist.)	8.4–9.5
12.5	9.5–12
12.5 (Fireline)	10.5–12
12.5 (moisture resist.)	11.2–12.7
19.0	14.0–17.5

Fig. 3.9   Recommended method of carrying plasterboard

Handling of plasterboard

When boards are manually off-loaded or stacked they should be carried on edge, two men to a board (see Fig. 3.9). Boards should never be carried with their surfaces horizontal since this imposes an undesirable strain on the core. When a board is handled, the long edge should be placed down before it is turned horizontal. Boards should not be dragged over each other as this can scuff the surface.

Storage of plasterboard

The boards should be stacked on a level surface in a dry place, preferably inside a building where they can be protected from damp and inclement weather (see Fig. 3.10). If they have to be stored outside, the stack must be out of contact with the ground, on a level platform and completely covered with a securely anchored polythene sheet or tarpaulin. A suitable platform can be constructed from timber bearers 100–125 mm wide, not less than the width of the boards in length and placed not more than 400 mm apart, at right angles to the length of the boards. Storage on bearers spaced wider than 400 mm may result in permanent deformation of the lower boards in a stack.

Storage of plasterboard on site is of paramount importance, as it is easily damaged by impact and can be ruined by water saturation.

Fig. 3.10   Recommended method of stacking plasterboard

Loading-out of plasterboard

If loading-out is done as a separate operation before the tacking, care must be taken not to overload upper floors which, in accordance with the Building Regulations, are designed in housing for a loading of 1.5 kN/m² (approximately 30 lb/ft²). Unless this is carefully monitored, labourers tend to put all the plaster board required for the first floor in one stack in the middle of the largest room, grossly overloading the floor and causing considerable deflection in the joists. Even after the load is removed, the joists seldom return to their original level. It is unwise to put more than fourteen sheets of 12.5 mm plasterboard (1200 × 240 mm) in any one stack.

Tacking of plasterboard

All four edges of a sheet of 9.5 or 12.5 mm plasterboard should be supported. On ceilings, noggings between joists should be inserted to support the edges and short ends, the boards always running at right angles to the run of the joists. The maximum centres of joists and studs to receive plasterboards are as follows:

09.5 mm thick   900 mm wide 450 mm max. centres
               1200 mm wide 400 mm max. centres
12.5 mm thick   900 mm wide 450 mm max. centres
               1200 mm wide 600 mm max. centres
19.0 mm thick   600 mm wide 600 mm max. centres
               (vertical)
               800 mm max centres (horizontal)

Ceilings must be tacked before walls the wallboards thus providing additional edge support to the ceiling boards. Fix the boards with the paper-covered edges lightly butted together and the short edges staggered. To walls, fix the boards with the paper-covered edges vertical and centred over a support. Alternatively, the boards may be fixed horizontally but noggings must be inserted to support the long edges. In all cases, cut ends must be located over a support and wherever possible should occur at internal angles. All boards should be nailed to every support at 150 mm centres working from the centre of the boards, outwards. The nails should be not less than 12 mm from ends and 10 mm from the bound edges of the boards, 30 × 2.60 mm and 40 × 2.60 mm Gyproc galvanized nails to fix 9.5 mm and 12.5 mm thick boards respectively. Nails should be driven home firmly without the head fracturing the paper surface but leaving a shallow depression to facilitate spotting. Approximately 5.5 kg of 30 mm nails or 5.7 kg of 40 mm nails are required for 100 m² of board. Some designers prefer to specify galvanized annular-ringed shank nails using the double-nailing technique. Instead of a single nail at 150 mm centres, two nails approximately 25 mm apart are inserted at 225 mm centres. This method is claimed to help avoid nail popping, i.e. where movement of the timber support causes the nails to protrude slightly on the finished face.

When two layers of plasterboard are to be fixed to timber framing, the spacing of the frame members and the nogging detail applies as for single-layer linings. All joints in the second layer must be staggered from those in the first. The nails for fixing the second layer must be 50 mm long.

Tacking is sometimes carried out by carpenters and sometimes by the jointers. It is best for the work to be done by the jointers if for no other reason than that it avoids a divided responsibility for a good complete dry-lining job. No matter how good everything else is in a building, if you have not achieved a good dry-lining finish you have not achieved a good job.

When fixing plasterboard to walls, care must be exercised to ensure that the boards are tight up to the ceiling boards and that there is a gap of approximately 15 mm between the bottom of the board and the top of the floor finish. This gap is most important as it prevents any water spillage on the floor soaking up into the plasterboard (see Fig. 3.11). Plasterboard to walls must be continuous, notwithstanding the fact that parts will be covered by baths, ducts, kitchen fittings, etc.

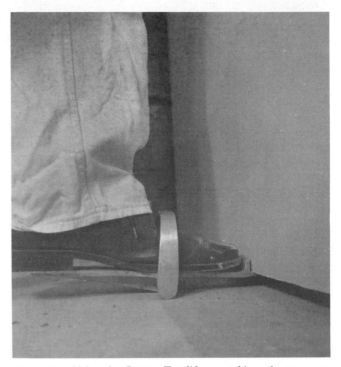

Fig. 3.11   Using the Gyproc Footlifter to achieve the necessary gap between bottom of plasterboard and floor level

When cutting boards around openings, vertical joints in line with reveals should be avoided. Generally speaking, plasterboard is a very tolerant material and, despite movement in timber frame construction, cracking in plasterboard surfaces is most unusual. If, however, plasterboard is jointed in line with a reveal of an opening, the weakest part of the plasterboard surface is over the position when most movement is likely to occur.

Tacking staircase wells needs careful consideration. It will be remembered that most shrinkage in a building occurs in the floor thickness zone as timber shrinks mostly in its width, i.e. the floor joists shrink in depth. Internally, this only affects the staircase well. Horizontal joints in the plasterboard in the floor joist zone of the staircase well should be left a little larger than elsewhere thus requiring more filler. The theory behind this is that when the joists shrink, the filler will be squeezed out and the filler is comparatively easy to rub down and redecorate. If boards are butted tightly together over the floor joist zone, they tend to bulge out and become unsightly when the joists shrink. Some designers provide for a timber waistband round the joist zone in staircase wells to cover the possible bulging of the plasterboard. A gap can then be left between the boards and covered on the surface by a timber waistband.

Early in the history of the modern timber frame in the UK, careful taking-off of plasterboard requirements for each room was the normal practice to take advantage of the full range of board sizes available. The exercise was to use boards of the maximum size and minimum waste to avoid cutting, taping and filling. The North American practice was followed of tacking wall plasterboard horizontally and this proved very successful. Vertical joints were minimal, as few walls were over 4.57 m (15 ft) long without an opening (15 ft long boards were then available with tapered edges and $\frac{1}{2}$ in thick). The one horizontal joint at mid-height becomes undetectable even with strong side lighting from a window at right angles. Today, it is very difficult to persuade dry-lining operatives to accept horizontal boarding, they prefer to keep to 1200 × 2400 mm and 1200 × 2350 mm boards fixed vertically to walls. With the greater use of dry-lining techniques, the tape and fill operatives have become most efficient in their work and, therefore, consider that the extra jointing created by vertical tacking is more economical than the extra work in fixing mid-height noggings, taking-off, ordering and loading-out involved in horizontal fixing to walls. It is strange that this does not appear to be the case in North America.

Jointing of plasterboard

Plasterboard ceilings to receive a texture coating finish such as Artex, should be in square-edged boards. The joints are taped by the Artex operatives but it should be made clear who is to tape the internal angle joint between walls and ceiling. Generally speaking, this should be done by whoever it is decided should carry out his work first, the Artex ceiling man or the jointer of the plasterboard walls, generally known as the tape-and-fill operation. Builders have differing views as to which is preferable.

Where more than one layer of plasterboard is used, all but the finishing layer can be square edged. All finishing layers should be tapered-edge boards to enable a first-class finish to be obtained. The jointing, or tape-and-fill operation, can be carried out manually or mechanically.

Manual jointing

Gyproc Jointex is the latest jointing compound developed by British Gypsum to make the hand-jointing of tapered-edge plasterboard a much easier and quicker operation. With Jointex, only one filling material is necessary but this material cannot be used in the Ames or any other proprietary make of mechanical jointing tool. Gyproc Jointex conforms to BS 6241 : 1982 – *Specification for Jointing Materials for Plasterboards*. It is a dual purpose compound being suitable for both bedding and finishing applications (Type 3) and is a gypsum-based setting compound (Class B).

Jointex is a compound with a composite, hemihydrate gypsum setting and air drying, hardening action. It is a compound for gap filling, tape bedding, filling, finishing and angle treatments in hand-jointing. It is supplied in 25 kg polythene bags with a shelf life of 6 months when stored under cover and in dry conditions.

Gyproc plasterboard surfaces jointed with Jointex are designated Class 0 as defined in the 1976 Building Regulations.

Approximate material requirements per 100 m² of dry lining to be hand jointed with Jointex are:

Jointex compound	40–45 kg
Joint tape	128–146 m
Drywall Top Coat	8–9 litres (1 coat)
	14–15 litres (2 coats)

Gyproc corner tape is supplied in 30 m rolls and angle beads in 2400 and 3000 mm lengths.

Jointex is mixed by sprinkling approximately 10 kg into 5 litres of clean water and stirring. Mixing should be carried out in well-ventilated conditions and the mixture should be allowed to stand for 10 minutes before final stirring into a thick creamy consistency. It should be used within approximately 90 minutes of mixing. It must not be retempered and any material that has begun to set before use, must be discarded.

Hand-jointing tapered-edge plasterboard with Jointex is divided into three operations as follows.

1 A continuous thin band of Jointex is applied to the taper at the board joints. Press the pre-cut lengths of joint tape into the band of Jointex using the taping knife (see Fig. 3.12), ensuring that the tape is firmly embedded and free from air bubbles but with sufficient Jointex left under the tape to ensure good adhesion. Allow to stand for a minimum of 5 minutes.

2 Another band of Jointex 200 mm wide is applied flush with the surface of the boards (see Fig. 3.13). Feather out the edges with the jointing sponge which should be kept moist and frequently rinsed to prevent any Jointex setting in it. At this stage, any obvious depressions in the surface should be filled and any projections removed.

Fig. 3.12 Jointex joint tape bedding

Fig. 3.13   Application of 200 mm wide band of Jointex

3 When the filling applications have been set and dried, a thin layer of Jointex 250–300 mm wide is applied over the joint. The edges are feathered out as before with a moist jointing sponge (see Fig. 3.14). When this is dry, the joints are lightly sanded to remove any minor imperfections.

Cut edges should ideally occur only at internal angles but when unavoidable, they should be treated as follows. Lightly sandpaper the edges to remove any burrs then fill the gap between the boards flush with the board surface using Jointex. When the filling has set, apply a thin layer of Jointex over the joint and bed the joint tape into this as tightly as possible leaving sufficient compound under the tape to ensure good adhesion. Allow the tape to stand for a minimum of 5 minutes then make two more applications of Jointex as described in (2) and (3) above.

Gaps between the boards at internal angles should be filled with Jointex. A thin layer of Jointex is applied to both sides of the angle. The joint tape is folded and pressed into the angle using the taping knife to bed the tape, making sure that air bubbles are removed. There must be sufficient Jointex left under the tape to ensure good adhesion. A thin layer of Jointex 75 mm wide should then be applied to each side of the angle and feathered out with the jointing sponge. When this has set and dried, apply another coat of Jointex 100 mm wide to both sides of the angle and feather the edges out with the jointing sponge.

When external angles are formed, any cut edge should be masked by a bound edge. External angles are reinforced with either Gyproc corner tape or Gyproc angle bead. Gyproc corner tape consists of a strong paper tape, 53 mm wide to which parallel steel reinforcement strips are bonded. When folded at the joint between the strips and applied correctly, it provides a straight, robust, external angle. Gyproc angle bead is a perforated galvanized steel angle strip, the arris being formed by a quarter-round metal bead which is left exposed to provide a very hard-wearing feature.

To apply Gyproc corner tape, first cut the tape to the length required and crease firmly at the centre to allow the steel strips to lie close to the plasterboard surfaces. Apply a 50 mm wide band of Jointex to each side of the angle with the taping knife. The corner tape should be pressed firmly on to the angle with the taping knife, making sure that the arris of the folded tape is straight

Fig. 3.14   Feathering out the edges with the Joint Sponge

Fig. 3.15   Bedding of Gyproc corner tape for the reinforcement of external angles

(see Fig. 3.15). Immediately after bedding the tape, apply a 150 mm band of Jointex to both sides of the angle and feather out the edges with a moist jointing sponge. After this has set and dried, a thin layer of Jointex 200 mm wide should be applied and the edges again feathered out with a Jointing sponge.

When maximum protection is required for the external angle, Gyproc angle bead should be used. It is fixed by applying a 50 mm wide band of Jointex to both sides of the angle with the taping knife. The angle bead is pressed firmly into place over the angle with the outer edges touching the plasterboard surface (see Fig. 3.16). Apply a 150 mm wide band of Jointex immediately and feather out with a moist jointing sponge. After this has set and dried, a thin layer 200 mm wide should be applied to both sides and the edges again feathered out with a moist jointing sponge.

Neither corner tape nor angle bead should be jointed but should run in one continuous piece from floor to ceiling.

Nail heads should be spotted, i.e. the depressions over the heads should be filled flush with the board surface. This should be done by two applications of Jointex, the first being allowed to set before the second is applied.

After the final jointing operation and before decoration, the whole surface should be lightly sanded, dusted down and treated with one coat of Gyproc Drywall Top Coat. Top Coat is applied with a roller and serves to even out the differences in surface texture and absorption between the board and jointed areas. It provides a consistent primed background for the first coat of paint, and when wallpapering, it provides a sealed surface and allows the wallpaper to be wet stripped when redecorating.

Mechanical jointing

Where there is a steady and reasonably large amount of work, jointing can be carried out with the Ames mechanical jointing tools.

Application. Joint cement for use with the Ames machine is supplied in powder form for site mixing or ready-mixed. The powder can be mixed in a large container and transferred to a smaller plastic container (335 mm deep) which can be emptied by the pump. The powder is sprinkled gradually into clean water and stirred with a mixing tool to a thick creamy consistence then allowed to stand for 30 minutes. More powder can be added to thicken the mixture if necessary. The approximate covering capacity of joint cement mixed on site is 40–50 kg/100 m². Ready-mixed joint cement needs only stirring on site before use. The approximate covering capacity of ready-mix joint cement is 55–70 kg/100 m². A hand pump is used to fill the auto-taper with joint cement.

When the auto-taper is run along the joints, it automatically dispenses the correct amount of joint cement and tape to tapered-edged joints and internal angles (see Figs. 3.17 and 3.18). External angles have to be jointed manually.

When the taping has dried, a coat of joint cement is applied with the 180 mm finisher (see Fig. 3.19) and allowed to dry. A further coat of joint cement is then applied using the 255 mm finisher followed after drying with a final coat using the 305 mm finisher.

The jointing of cut edges is carried out as described

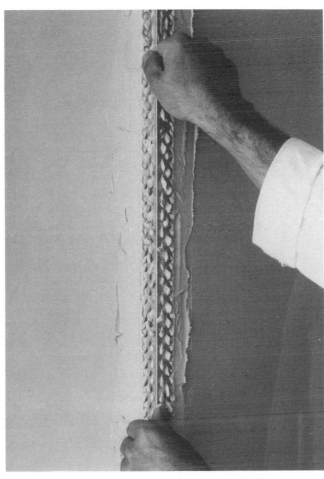

Fig. 3.16 *Bedding of Gyproc angle bead for maximum protection to external angles*

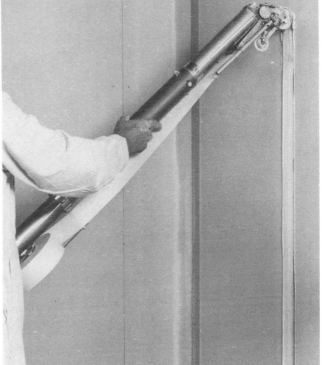

Fig. 3.17 *Tape and fill by the Ames mechanical jointing tools – application of tape and cement by auto-taper*

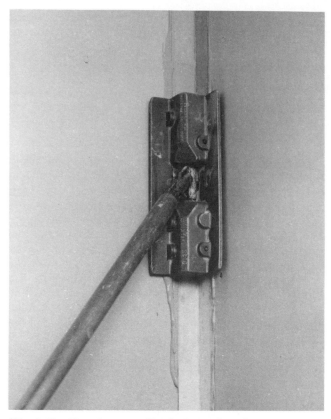

Fig. 3.18   *Use of corner roller for internal angles*

Fig. 3.19   *Application of layer of joint cement with 180 mm finisher*

above after taking the same preparatory action as for manual jointing.

The Ames tools include a mechanical nail spotter but experience shows that the experienced tape-and-fill operative prefers to fill the nail holes by hand.

The surface finish is as for hand-jointing.

Protection.   When the Ames tools are used, the operatives keep the various parts in water, contained either in a plastic dustbin or 50 gallon drum. In cold weather and for reasons of security of their equipment, they tend to keep this equipment inside a house, where they also mix their jointing compounds. All this can cause a lot of water spillage and mess. Site management should insist from the beginning of a job that, where these operations take place, the floor of the house is adequately protected.

Ducts

Ducts are sometimes provided to conceal plumbing and SVPs. It is essential to finish these ducts in plasterboard to avoid the differential movement and subsequent cracking bound to occur where the duct face meets the wall when the duct is finished in plywood. Plywood is often specified for this position because of the comparative ease of providing removable access panels. However, access panels can also be provided in plasterboard with a little careful detailing thus avoiding those unsightly gaps that occur when finished wall surface meets plywood duct at right angles.

Plasterboard is a strong, tolerant and fire-resistant material but must be handled, stored and fixed with respect and care.

Tools used in dry lining

British Gypsum market a full range of tools for the dry liner. Among the most commonly used are the following.

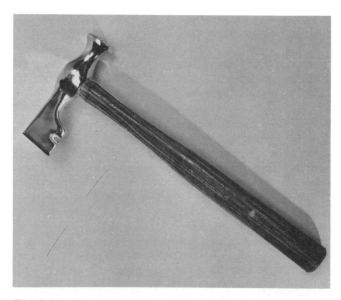

Fig. 3.20   *Wood-shafted dry-wall hammer with rounded and chequered head*

Tacker's hammer (reference G2), see Fig. 3.20.   Has a rounded, slightly domed and chequered head enabling the tacker to drive the nails home slightly below the surface without breaking the paper finish and providing a key for the nail filling.

Footlifter (reference G4), see Fig. 3.11.   A simple gadget for lifting wallboards slightly off the floor with the foot, leaving both hands free for tacking.

Fig. 3.21 Wallboard trimmer. Trims up to 112 mm off wallboards quickly and neatly

Wallboard trimmer (reference U1), see Fig. 3.21. Trims up to 112 mm off wallboards quickly and neatly. The steel wheels perforate both sides of the board so that it can be snapped off cleanly. It has a depth scale on one edge.

Jointing sponge (reference J1), see Fig. 3.14. A circular plastic sponge with plastic handle. Used at all stages of jointing to clean off surplus material, feather the edges and give final finish.

200 mm applicator (reference J2). A 200 mm rigid blade with plastic grip for applying joint filler and joint finish by hand.

Long-handled broad knife (reference A1), see Fig. 3.22. A 175 mm blade to flatten joint tape and remove any excess cement. Has a long handle enabling most wiping to be carried out from the floor. Used with Ames mechanical jointing tools.

Universal sander (reference A3), see Fig. 3.28. Long-handled sander with universal joint at head so that ceiling and wall joints can be sanded from the floor. Used with Ames mechanical jointing tools.

Ames mechanical jointing tools. These are available only from British Gypsum who hire the following items: loading pump with goose-neck; auto-taper, 180, 225 and 305 mm finishers; corner roller; 76 mm corner finisher with cement container and the nail spotter. Other accessories are sold.

Before Ames jointing tools are hired out, operatives are given full training in their use by British Gypsum. This consists of one week at the Product Training Centre at Erith, Kent or Carlisle, Cumbria and at least one week on site.

Internal finishes

Finishes to internal walls and ceilings can be identical to those used in masonry construction. Indeed, in some instances, finishes are much easier to apply in timber frame construction. A 1200 × 2400 mm decorative

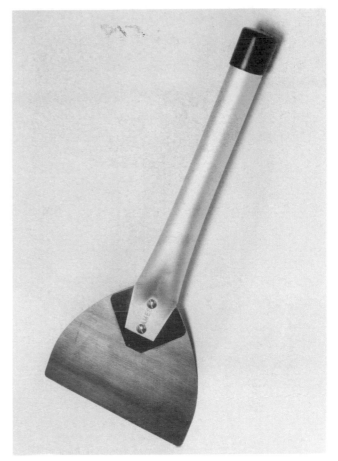

Fig. 3.22 Long-handled broad knife. 175 mm replaceable blade used to flatten joint tape and remove any excess cement

Fig. 3.23 Universal sander. Long-handled sander with universal joint at head enabling ceiling and wall joints to be sanded from the floor

panelling of sheet plywood is a good example, as it can be applied direct to the plasterboard, whereas, with masonry construction and wet plaster, battens would have to be applied and shimmed out to a true and level surface to receive the panelling.

The finishes to the plasterboard surfaces should be applied as soon as possible after the jointing has dried to prevent the plasterboard from soaking up any moisture vapour in the air.

Emulsion paint

Emulsion paint to dry-lined wall surfaces is probably most commonly used and gives a good serviceable

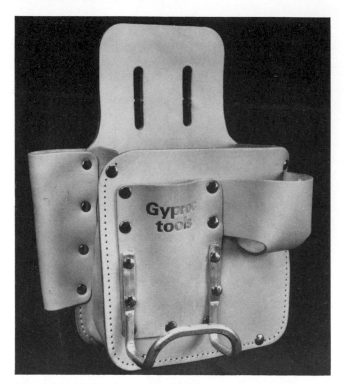

Fig. 3.24 Nail pouch and tool holder

finish. However, great care must be taken to ensure that the correct emulsion paint is used. Most paint manufacturers produce an emulsion paint which they market especially for first-time application on new plaster. They claim, quite correctly, that this emulsion paint, besides being cheaper, allows the wet plaster to dry out through the paint surface. With timber frame construction and dry-wall linings, the problem of allowing the wet plaster to dry out through the paint does not apply and the first-time application emulsion is unnecessary. It should not be used if a first-class job is required because, although it is cheaper and covers well, it is not washable and is easily removed when occupiers try to remove dirty marks from walls.

Experience has shown that best results are achieved with emulsion paint when it is applied with a mohair roller. For most neutral colours, two-coat application will suffice. If dark colours or brilliant white are used, an additional coat may be required to obliterate completely the joints in the plasterboard.

Ceiling finishes

Patent decorative ceiling finishes, such as Artex, are commonly used and are generally carried out by a specialist subcontractor. Artex AX is a decorative finish for use on interior surfaces to achieve a wide variety of textured patterns. It contains no asbestos but consists of water-soluble binders combined with inert fillers and pigments and incorporates a fungicide. It can be applied to most commonly used building surfaces but is only available in white. Application is by brush, roller or spray gun and a wide range of different patterned textures is available. Artex AX is reinforced and will resist cracking associated with normal building movement. It is a permanent finish designed to last the lifetime of the background to which it is applied. The covering capacity for a textured finish is approximately 2.5 m²/kg.

Square-edged plasterboard can be used to receive Artex and the taping of the joints is part of the specialist's operation.

Wallpaper

Wallpaper may be applied to dry-lined plasterboard provided the plasterboard first receives a coat of sealer to facilitate ultimate removal of the wallpaper without injuring the paper finish to the plasterboard surface. All paint manufacturers will advise on their recommended sealer for this work or Gyproc Drywall Top Coat by British Gypsum may be used.

Oil-bound point

Oil-bound paint is sometimes specified for bathrooms and kitchens. A sealer coat is beneficial where dark colours or brilliant white is specified, whereas two coats of oil-bound paint in neutral colours will normally suffice without the sealer.

Painting generally

It should always be remembered that, with all forms of painting, the cost of the materials is a comparatively small proportion of the total cost of the work. It is, therefore, a false economy not to use a good quality paint.

Chapter 4
Exterior finishes

Exterior finishes, both to walls and roofs, fulfil the functions of weatherproofing the structure, creating a pleasing appearance and providing the necessary fire resistance to the timber structure as required by the Building Regulations. Exterior finishes to walls are never structural in that they do not support the floors and roofs. The timber frame is the complete structural element in itself. Exterior finishes are either supported by the timber frame (tile hanging, rendering, roof tiling, etc.) or in the case of brick cladding, are self-supporting and merely tied back to the timber frame for stability.

Claddings

Brick cladding

This is the most popular cladding in use in the UK no doubt because it requires virtually no maintenance and has stood the test of time. It is applied single-leaf thick with a cavity, usually 50 mm, between brickwork and timber frame. The brickwork is tied back to the timber frame with flexible stainless steel brick ties which are nailed with two 30 mm square twisted nails through into each stud at every fifth course of brickwork (see Fig. 4.1). The lower of the two nails must be located as near as possible to the bend of the brick tie. Stainless steel nails must be used with the stainless steel brick ties.

It is normal to have the bricklayer responsible for nailing the ties in position as he progresses with his brickwork. This sometimes needs some persuasion as it is unusual to ask a bricklayer to use a hammer and nails in the course of his work. It is also a stage of the work that needs extra-special supervision as the work proceeds because it is almost impossible to check whether the right number of brick ties have been used in the correct places after the brickwork is completed.

When detailing brickwork, it must be remembered that the timber frame will shrink while the brickwork, which is self-supporting, will not. Therefore the top of the brickwork cladding must always stop short of the underside of gable ladders, trusses forming eaves overhangs, etc. A gap of at least 10–12 mm should be left between the top of brickwork and the underside of any timber forming part of, or fixed to, the timber frame structure (see Fig. 4.2).

Section 8 of Practice Note No. 5 (1982) of the NHBC, besides illustrating the positions where allowances must be made for differential movement between dissimilar materials, gives the following table of shrinkage allowances for platform frame construction:

	Suspended timber GF when panels are supported on GF joists or perimeter joists	Other GF constructions
Allow. for GF openings	5 mm	3 mm
Allow. for 1st F openings	12 mm	9 mm
Allow. for 2nd F openings	18 mm	15 mm
Eaves and verges	Add 3 mm to the allowance for openings on that floor	

Fig. 4.1 Brick cladding showing brick ties in place

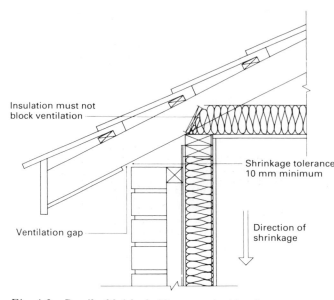

Fig. 4.2   *Detail of brick cladding to underside of trusses*

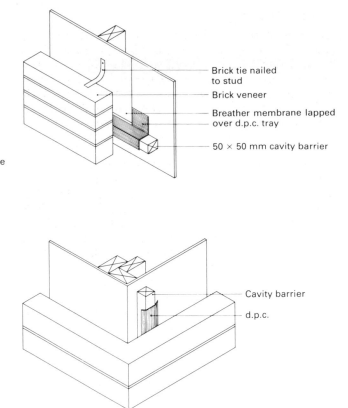

Fig. 4.3   *Dpc covering to timber cavity barriers*

Vertical joints should be left open and clear at 1500 mm centres in the course of brickwork immediately below the dpc to allow free circulation of air behind the brick cladding and so allow the timber frame to breathe. Similar open joints should be provided below horizontal cavity barriers at eaves and verge level.

In long terraces of houses with continuous clay-brick cladding, care must be taken to provide expansion joints in the brickwork at every 12 m. If there are projections or staggers on plan, a straight vertical joint can easily and unobtrusively be provided in the corner of the internal angle. With a completely flat elevation a 10 mm wide straight joint filled with mastic behind the rainwater downpipe is a good way of complying with the recommendations of BRE Digest No. 65 – *The Selection of Clay Building Bricks*.

Cavity barriers have to be inserted in the cavity in certain positions laid down by the Building Regulations. Generally speaking, these are around all openings, horizontally at joist, verge and eaves level and vertically to break up large areas of cavity, i.e. at external corners of buildings and where the unbroken width of cavity exceeds 8 m. The material used for the cavity barriers is usually non-combustible cavity-fill quilt which must not be confused with a similar-looking material used for roof insulation and known as insulation quilt. Horizontal cavity barriers at joist level have to be covered with a cavity tray dressed up the face of the breather membrane. It is recommended that the cavity-fill material is fixed in its correct positions by a carpenter or labourer immediately before the bricklayer begins. The same principle applies to the fire stopping at separating and compartment walls. It is unreasonable to expect the bricklayer to fix the cavity barriers and fire stopping as he proceeds. Indeed, very careful supervision is needed to ensure that these are not dislodged or even removed by the bricklayer as he works.

Cavity barriers can also be timber battens the full depth of the cavity. They must be of preserved timber and protected from moisture by a dpc between cladding and timber, both horizontally and vertically, as laid down in Clauses 4.4.c. V and VI of of NHBC Practice Note No. 5 (see Fig. 4.3). However, as a 50 mm cavity is allowed a plus 10 and minus 15 mm tolerance (Clause 4.4.c. of NHBC Practice Note No. 5), it will be seen that a 50 mm thick timber cavity barrier can cause problems if the cavity decreases in width and becomes non-effective if it increases in width.

These cavity barriers apply to all claddings not directly fixed to the sheathing, i.e. all claddings fixed to battens applied to the sheathing and, of course, masonry.

Weep holes should be provided over all external joinery openings as for traditional construction.

Only overall dimensions of the brickwork are required to be shown on the drawings because the timber frame with its built-in openings for windows and doors provides a template for the bricklayer to work to. Careful setting-out by the bricklayer before he commences laying is, however, most important. He should plumb down from the upper windows to ensure that the reveals are, in fact, dead in line if that is what is required by the drawings. He must also check distances between joinery items to see how they will affect his bonding, because modules of measurement used in timber frame design do not always suit brick dimensions. Coursing must be checked to ensure that window sills and heads are met correctly. Unlike masonry construction, windows are set in position before the bricklayer commences. He is, therefore, set a different problem, with which the good designer will help by providing the correct dimensioned heights of sills and heads. The importance for the timber frame structure to be plumb and true soon becomes apparent when the brick cladding rises. What starts off as a 50 mm cavity at the bottom can disappear or double in size by the time the bricklayer reaches second-floor level if the structure is not plumb. This will, of course, produce serious problems where the brickwork passes projecting window and door frames set in the timber frame and the cavity barriers fixed to the timber frame.

Timber cladding

Any form of timber cladding may be used, vertical, horizontal or diagonal. It is generally applied to 22 × 38 mm treated battens fixed at right angles to the finished boarding except for diagonal boarding where the battens can be either vertical or horizontal. In all cases, the battens must be secured through into the studs. With vertical cladding and horizontal battens, care should be taken to leave 10–20 mm gaps between butt ends of the battens to ensure a circulation of air between breather paper and back of cladding.

Non-durable hardwoods and softwoods, with the exception of Western Red Cedar and Californian Redwood, should be pressure treated with CCA preservative which may be left to weather naturally or finished with a water repellant stain or micro-porous paint. Boards may be saw-textured or planed with a minimum thickness of 16 mm which may be reduced to 6.5 mm at the thin edge of tapered boards. Only one nail per board is used at fixings and nails must be corrosion-resistant, galvanized, aluminium or sherardized.

Timber cladding at upper-floor level over brickwork at ground floor is a very common combination in the UK. Great care must be taken in detailing the joint where the two claddings meet. As well as an adequate flashing to cover the projection of the brickwork, provision must be allowed for the timber floor joists to shrink and the timber cladding which is attached to the frame to come down. A gap of a minimum of 10–12 mm must therefore be left between top of brickwork and underside of timber battens and cladding (see Fig. 4.4).

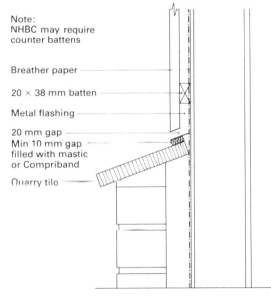

Fig. 4.4   Timber cladding above brick cladding

Tile hanging

Horizontal battens fixed as for vertical boarding are essential for tile hanging. Apart from this, there is absolutely no difference from tile hanging on masonry. Where tile hanging occurs above brickwork some designers have successfully used timber sprockets at the junction of the two so that the bottom course of tiles overlaps the top of the brickwork and eliminates the need for a flashing as mentioned in the previous paragraph (see Fig. 4.5). The 10–12 mm gap between top of brickwork and underside of sprockets is, of course, still required. The use of sprockets works well for infill

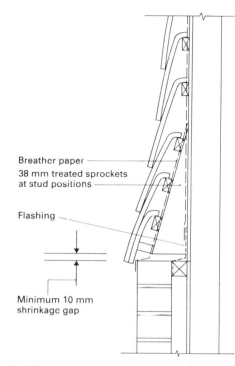

Fig. 4.5   Tile hanging on sprockets above brick cladding

panels but complications are met at external corners and it can become quite unsightly.

Rendering

Rendering is normally applied to some form of patent lathing fixed to battens as for the other claddings previously mentioned. The best types of lathing are those that incorporate a waterproof paper back to the galvanized wire mesh. This backing prevents the filling of the cavity created by the battens behind the lathing. By maintaining the cavity the insulation value of the external wall is increased and, incidentally, material saved, thus decreasing the weight and cost.

Great care should be taken in fixing the lathing, which must always be carried out strictly in accordance with manufacturers' instructions. Apparent little points are sometimes missed, such as the twisting together of the wires when joining sheets of lathing. So often they are just lapped. With Twil Lath, it is also important to see that the galvanized wires that have a thin stainless steel wire wrapped round them are used as fixing wires. Rust-resisting staples must always be used for fixing.

Render on lathing on battens, provided it is applied correctly, can be a very effective cladding (see Fig. 4.6). However, the most vulnerable position for a defect is at external angles. Operatives tend to bend the lathing through 90° by hand and, therefore, do not get a sharp angle, with consequent loss of rendering material which is applied with a true 90° angle. Where this occurs, cracking often appears. The lathing must be hammered to a true and sharp 90° or a special corner reinforcement lath utilized.

It must be realized that extensive rendering on a timber frame housing contract can delay completions considerably. The fixings of battens and lathing is followed by two, and sometimes three, separate and distinct operations with a drying-out time after each. Each of these operations is controlled by weather conditions. High winds causing dust to fly, hot sun, frost and rain all hold up progress. It will also be real-

Fig. 4.6   Render on Twil Lath AX metal lathing over brick ground-floor cladding

ized that scaffolding is utilized for a much longer period than for any other form of cladding.

Maximum areas of rendering without expansion joints are set out in BS 5262 : 1976. Where vertical expansion joints are required, they are best located behind rainwater pipes wherever possible. Horizontal slip joints, where required, should coincide with the floor joist area, i.e. where most shrinkage of the timber frame is liable to take place.

Some designers may prefer to apply rendering to brickwork or blockwork cladding. When this is done, great care must be taken in detailing to ensure that the rendering does not meet window and door frames in the reveals of openings. Differential movement between the timber frame and the masonry will inevitably cause cracking unless steps are taken to keep these two elements apart. This can be achieved by inserting a piece of hardboard strip temporarily between the end of the render and the joinery frame. When the render is set, the hardboard strips should be withdrawn and the gaps left behind sealed with a mastic to allow for the differential movement between the timber frame and the rendering.

Sheet materials

Any form of exterior quality sheet material finished in a variety of ways can be used for relatively small infill panels usually above and below windows. Battens for these panels are fixed all as previously described for timber cladding. Great care must be taken to see that the edges of the sheets are well protected and that there is a watertight flashing between sheets and adjacent claddings and, if these are of masonry, allowance must be made for differential movement.

Patent claddings

Stove-enamelled aluminium or steel siding, asbestos cement shingles, plastic siding, etc. can all be used if fixed to manufacturers' instructions but, again, the same strict caution must be exercised where two different claddings meet on the same plane.

Roof coverings

Roof coverings for both flat and pitched roofs can be identical to those used in traditional construction and can be detailed in exactly the same way with one exception. That exception is where a flat or pitched roof is penetrated by masonry – a chimney for example – or where a flat or pitched roof abuts a masonry wall – a ground-floor projection or an attached flat-roofed garage for example. The problem of differential movement has again to be solved. Unlike the masonry, the timber frame is liable to move with the shrinkage of timber. This problem is overcome by a double flashing, one dressed over the roof tiles and laid up against the brickwork and one dressed into the brickwork and coming down over the other allowing a good overlap (see Fig. 4.7). With flat roofs, instead of a bottom flashing, the upstand of the roof covering will suffice. This form of double flashing is known as counterflashing.

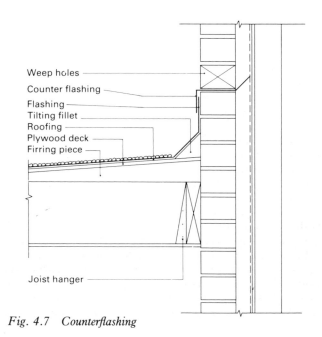

Weep holes
Counter flashing
Flashing
Tilting fillet
Roofing
Plywood deck
Firring piece

Joist hanger

Fig. 4.7   Counterflashing

Chapter 5
Special design considerations

Party walls

Party or compartment walls are required to provide adequate resistance to the passage of fire and sound from one dwelling to an adjoining one. Since 1966, as a result of extensive laboratory and field tests, timber-framed walls have been satisfying these functions in England and Wales and more recently approved in Scotland for houses, flats and maisonettes up to three storeys high. In general terms adequate fire resistance may be construed as meaning a full one-hour rating which can be achieved with two layers of 12.5 mm gypsum wallboard. In order to accommodate the requirements for sound transmission loss the overall thickness of the plasterboard on each side of the party wall is increased to a minimum of 32 mm and non-combustible batt insulation is installed to reduce sound transmission at certain frequencies. As a result timber-framed party walls built in accordance with the principles outlined in this section provide better fire resistance than the regulations require and they also have a better performance in terms of sound transmission loss than is required. Although the regulations do not cover the subject of impact sound, in this regard the spatial separation of timber-framed party walls provide a more than satisfactory performance as a bonus.

It is possible to incorporate brick or block party walls in timber-framed structures but this practice is not recommended since it introduces a wet trade into an otherwise dry construction technique with attendant differential movement problems. There is also the likelihood that the introduction of masonry will interfere with the time schedule for the erection of the timber frame components.

Construction

Timber-framed party walls are constructed as two walls separated by a minimum space of 250 mm between the backs of 32 mm plasterboard and 220 mm between the backs of 38 mm plasterboard. The fire resistance is achieved by the application of horizontal gypsum plank with vertically applied gypsum wallboard providing the finish. It is important to ensure that the integrity of the fire resistance is fully maintained from the foundations through to the roof finish and that particular care is taken in the roof space to ensure that the gypsum board is fully supported and the joints are covered. At each floor level, at the ceiling level and the roof level the cavity between the walls has non-combustible barriers installed to prevent the passage of fire and smoke, and additional members, either timber or non-combustible sheet materials, are installed in the floor structure to achieve the required fire resistance. Vertical fire stops are installed at the junction between the party wall cavity and external walls. The resistance to the passage of sound is achieved not by the density of the wall but by the spatial separation of the two components.

Because there are no structural members connecting the plasterboard linings, sound vibrations picked up by the diaphragm on one side are not readily transmitted to the other. For the reason, although the two walls are connected with metal straps located above the joist level they should not be spaced closer than 1.2 m centres (see Fig. 5.1).

Services in party walls

Plumbing and drainage services should not be installed in party walls. Where electrical services are installed in the wall service boxes should not be placed back to back and care must be taken to box them in to maintain the fire and sound integrity of the party wall (see Fig. 5.2). Sound can travel from one dwelling to another most easily through cracks and while it is not a mandatory requirement the sound performance of the timber-framed party wall can be improved if the bottom rail of the wall components is installed over a bead of acoustic sealant, or a strip of compressible plastic foam.

Timber compartment floors

Compartment floors separate one dwelling unit, whether a flat or maisonette, from another, and are required to meet a stipulated performance standard in terms of fire resistance and sound transmission. In addition to resisting the passage of airborne sound, impact sound must also be accommodated. Generally a full one-hour fire resistance is required although two-storey flats in England and Wales require only half-hour resistance. In practice it is found that in order to achieve the requirements for sound transmission loss, the thickness of the plasterboard ceiling lining will be increased to the point of providing one-hour fire resistance. It is very important to ensure that floors with one-hour fire resistance must be supported on load-bearing walls or partitions that also have one-hour fire resistance.

The requirement for impact sound resistance as well as resistance to the passage of airborne sound introduces some difficulties in meeting the requirements of the regulations and any method adopted should be supported by a certificate showing that the floor construction has been tested in accordance with BS 2570. Any deviation from an accepted method could have a significant effect on performance and a high level of site supervision is essential. In principle, airborne sound transmission is controlled by the spatial separation of the floor and ceiling diaphragms, and impact sound by providing what is essentially a cushion to absorb the sound of impact. Suggested methods of meeting the requirements are shown in Figs. 5.3–5.5 and the designer should note that while the Canadian and the Timber Research and Development Association (TRADA) methods allow the standard schedule of platform frame construction to be followed, the Swedish

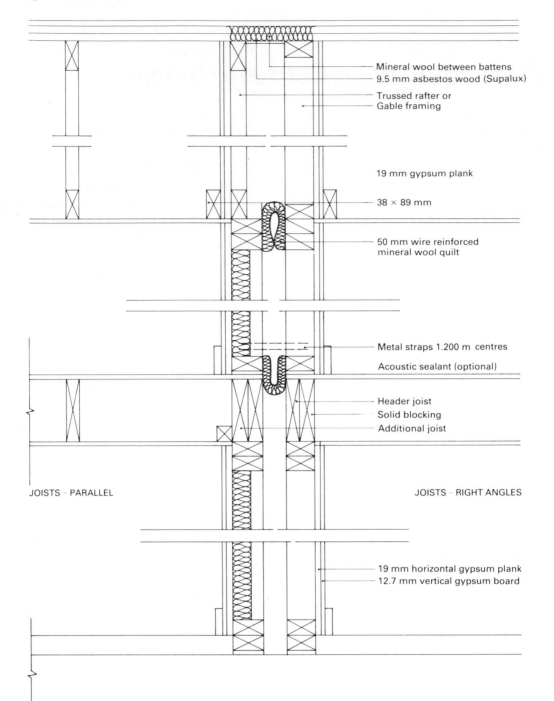

Fig. 5.1   Separating wall

- Mineral wool between battens
- 9.5 mm asbestos wood (Supalux)
- Trussed rafter or Gable framing

19 mm gypsum plank

38 × 89 mm

50 mm wire reinforced mineral wool quilt

Metal straps 1.200 m centres

Acoustic sealant (optional)

- Header joist
- Solid blocking
- Additional joist

JOISTS – PARALLEL

JOISTS – RIGHT ANGLES

19 mm horizontal gypsum plank
12.7 mm vertical gypsum board

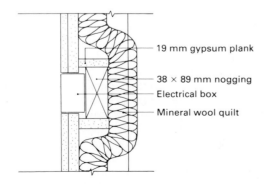

19 mm gypsum plank
38 × 89 mm nogging
Electrical box
Mineral wool quilt

Fig. 5.2   Electrical outlet in separating wall

method requires the building to be weathertight before the installation of the floors. The Canadian method of using a resilient sandwich to absorb the impact sound and either a separate ceiling construction or the resilient clips shown in the diagram offers the best compromise between structural integrity and acoustic performance. As with all sound-resisting elements of construction, the passage of air must be eliminated at all points by acoustic sealants.

Swedish – Finnish method

This system has been widely used and tested and has been shown to provide a consistently satisfactory performance providing that the battens are not nailed through to the joists. Junctions between the floor and load-bearing partitions require close attention and specialist advice should be obtained (see Fig. 5.3).

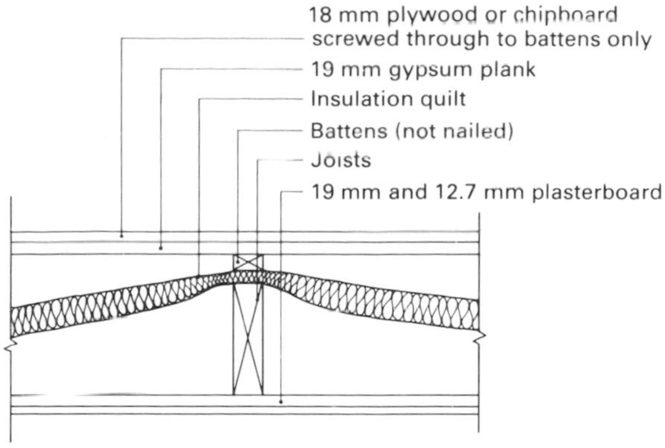
18 mm plywood or chipboard screwed through to battens only
19 mm gypsum plank
Insulation quilt
Battens (not nailed)
Joists
19 mm and 12.7 mm plasterboard

Fig. 5.3 Compartment floor, Swedish/Finnish method

Canadian method

This method does conform to platform frame techniques and relies on resilient metal clips supporting the ceiling battens to provide the spatial separation. This could also be achieved by a proprietary resilient metal channel to which the plasterboard is screwed (see Fig. 5.4). The Canadians commonly provide a floor finish of 50 mm of aerated concrete over a layer of impregnated bitumen board but this has not yet been tested in the UK.

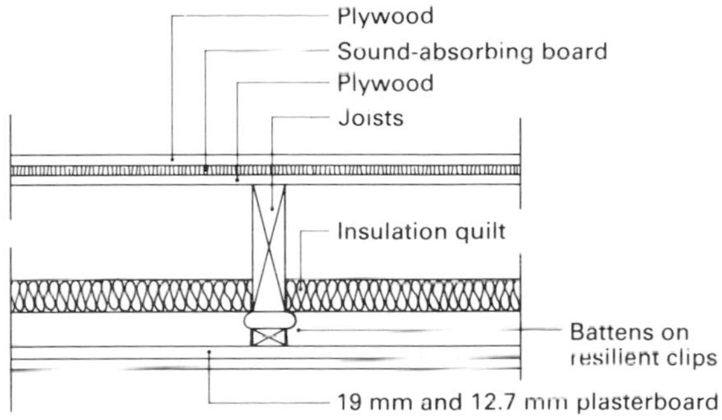
Plywood
Sound-absorbing board
Plywood
Joists
Insulation quilt
Battens on resilient clips
19 mm and 12.7 mm plasterboard

Fig. 5.4 Compartment floor, Canadian method

TRADA method

This has been developed by TRADA from a system common in North America where the floor and ceiling framing members are independent of each other. Further information on the details of this technique are available from TRADA (see Fig. 5.5).

Note: The approved document E – Sound amplifies and explains the requirements of the Building Regulations 1985 and provides further details on the methods of construction which may be deemed to satisfy these requirements.

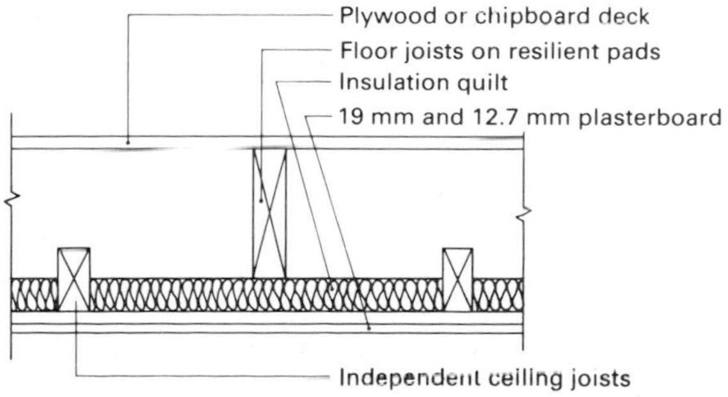
Plywood or chipboard deck
Floor joists on resilient pads
Insulation quilt
19 mm and 12.7 mm plasterboard
Independent ceiling joists

Fig. 5.5 Compartment floor, TRADA method

Sound transmission within dwellings

The passage of sound from one dwelling to another is effectively controlled by properly constructed timber-framed party walls and floors. Within modern dwellings regardless of the basic construction method adopted, the partitions tend to be of lightweight construction and in certain areas it may be desirable to improve the acoustic performance. Good planning will tend to separate noisy areas such as living rooms and bathrooms from quiet areas such as bedrooms. The average sound transmission loss in a timber-framed partition lined with 12.5 mm plasterboard is approximately 34 dB and some methods of increasing the sound transmission loss are listed below. As noted in the section on party walls, air gaps can be critical and the use of well-fitted doors and acoustic sealants under the bottom rails of partitions goes a long way towards improving the sound performance. Full height cupboards installed between rooms also provide a useful sound barrier.

Partition construction

Staggered studs

Using 38 × 145 mm (nom. 2 × 6) rails, studs at 600 mm centres are staggered as indicated in Fig. 5.6 and insulation quilt placed between the studs. The two 12.5 mm plasterboard linings have a space separation similar to that found in party walls. Using this method the approximate sound transmission loss is 44 dB.

Resilient metal channels

Proprietary metal channels are fixed to a standard timber wall frame and the plasterboard wall lining is fixed to it with self-tapping screws. The channels are flexible and much of the sound energy is absorbed and not transmitted from one diaphragm to the other. Further information on this technique is available from British Gypsum. When properly installed the sound transmission loss is similar to the staggered stud partition.

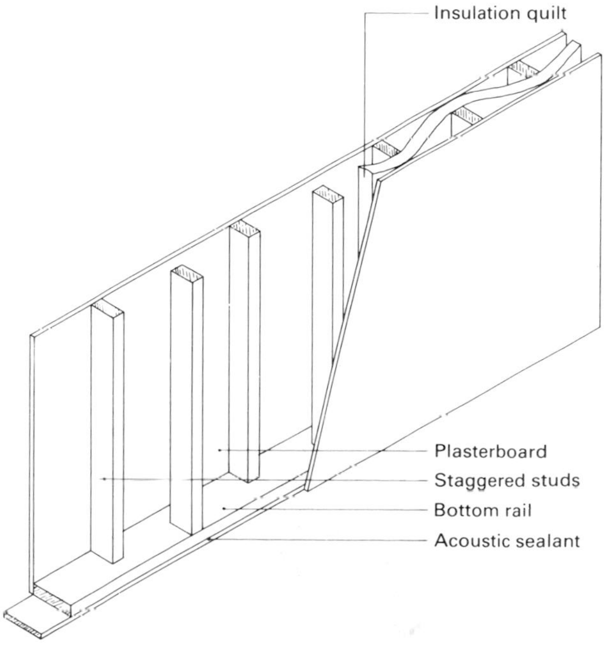
Insulation quilt
Plasterboard
Staggered studs
Bottom rail
Acoustic sealant

Fig. 5.6 Acoustic partition, staggered studs

Mismatched diaphragms

This method relies on the technique of mismatching the two diaphragms so that they will have different critical frequencies of vibration, and although not quite as effective as the other two methods it is quite simple and economic. One side of a standard timber frame partition has a simple layer of 12.5 mm plasterboard. On the other side, the plasterboard is bonded to an intermediate layer of either 12.5 mm plasterboard or insulation board (Fig. 5.7).

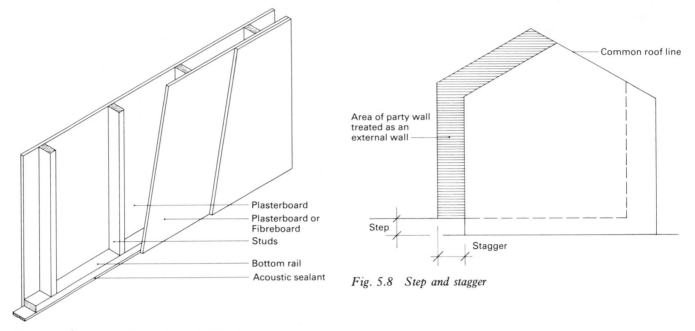

Fig. 5.7 Acoustic partition, mismatched diaphragm

Fig. 5.8 Step and stagger

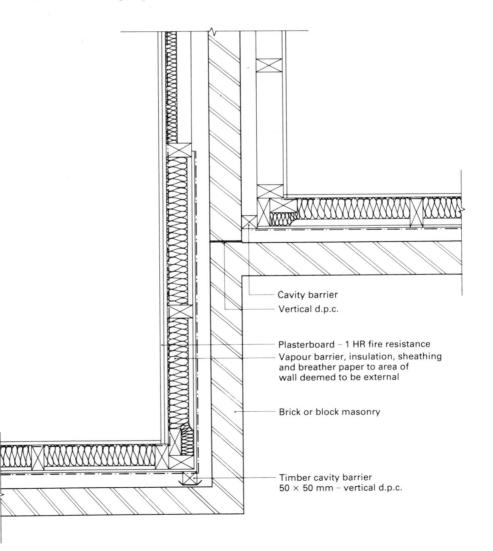

Fig. 5.9 Brick veneer detail for step and stagger

External noise

Noise penetrating into a dwelling from the exterior is very much the consequence of air leakage or crackage around openings rather than the method of construction. In any situation where a dwelling adjoins a noisy area such as a main road, openings should be kept to a reasonable minimum and should be double glazed and weatherstripped to reduce the passage of sound.

Steps and staggers

Steps and staggers in terraces of timber-framed houses do not present any particular problems, but careful attention to detail is necessary to ensure that the requirements of Building Regulations are met in respect of the fire resistance of the party wall. If the external finish of the party wall where it is exposed by the step or stagger is brick or block veneer as indicated in Fig. 5.8, provision must be made within the thickness of party wall to support the veneer through to the foundations. Figure 5.9 shows a typical detail which can be used to meet the requirements of the regulations. The area of party wall exposed is effectively an exterior wall built on the boundary. As such it requires a one-hour fire resistance from the interior, a minimum of 25 mm of plasterboard and also a one-hour fire resistance from the exterior. Previously stated requirements for thermal insulation must also be met (see also Fig. 6.1).

Where lightweight exterior finishes to the exposed areas are specified they may be supported directly by the timber frame but the same requirements for fire resistance and non-combustibility apply. Figure 5.10 indicates one alternative to masonry with a cladding of non-combustible clay tiles over a fire-resistant sheathing. Cement render on expanded metal lath could also be used to comply with the regulations. Where steps occur the cavity barrier installed at floor and ceiling levels must effectively seal the cavity as shown in Fig. 5.11.

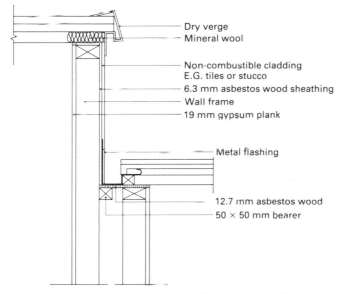

Dry verge
Mineral wool

Non-combustible cladding
E.G. tiles or stucco
6.3 mm asbestos wood sheathing
Wall frame
19 mm gypsum plank

Metal flashing

12.7 mm asbestos wood
50 × 50 mm bearer

Fig. 5.10   Lightweight cladding detail to exposed gable wall caused by step

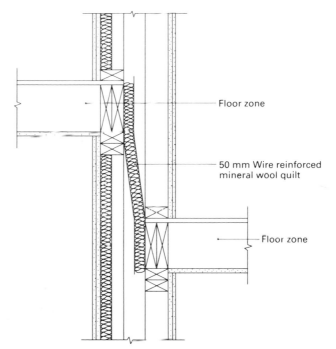

Floor zone

50 mm Wire reinforced mineral wool quilt

Floor zone

Fig. 5.11   Separating wall detail showing difference in level of joists caused by step

Chapter 6
Obtaining tenders

Individual units such as one-off houses

The owner of a plot of land desirous of building a timber-framed building thereon will no doubt employ the services of an architect or designer. An alternative is to approach a builder who will undertake to be responsible for the design, obtaining all necessary approvals and to build the building for an all-in lump sum price.

In the former case, the architect's or designer's role is, of course, exactly the same as when he is involved with a traditionally constructed building. If he is not experienced in timber frame construction, he might seek the advice of a timber frame manufacturer or of a timber frame consultant. If he goes to the manufacturer, the manufacturer will at least want his name specified in the tender documents as the supplier of the timber frame components. In some cases, the same firm may also want to be specified as the supplier of the joinery – windows, doors, staircase, etc. If he goes to a timber frame consultant, a fee will be payable which might be paid by the designer or passed on to the client in which case the designer's fee to the client should be reduced. The advantage of using a consultant is that you are then free to obtain competitive tenders from contractors without restricting the tenderers to one specified supplier of the timber frame components.

In order to obtain truly competitive tenders from more than one builder, it is therefore essential to have the following tender documents:

(a) Tender form;
(b) Site layout and site location drawing;
(c) Fully detailed drawings;
(d) Contract conditions proposed;
(e) Specification of the works;
(f) Manufacturing specification for the timber frame components;
(g) Erection specification.

Tender form

This should be clear and concise and leave only the sum of money to be inserted plus the contractor's signature. It should be clearly stated that no qualified tender will be acceptable and unless the tender form states the date for possession and date for completion, the tenderer must be able to quote his construction period.

Site layout and site location drawings

These must be adequately dimensioned and show sufficient finished levels. A site survey showing existing levels, existing drainage, bench mark, existing overhead or underground services, boundaries and site access points is of great help to tenderers.

Fully detailed drawings

Generally speaking, too many drawings cannot be given to a tenderer. The only reservation to this generality is that the more drawings there are, the more likelihood there is of the same detail being repeated not necessarily in the same way. Repetition of detail is therefore to be avoided.

Contract conditions proposed

This should be quoted together with any amendments proposed thereto and with full details of what is proposed to be inserted in the various apppendices.

Specification for the works

Besides containing the normal items as for traditional construction it should contain reference to all the points made in this book to the differences between timber frame construction and traditional masonry construction. Items to cover include:

(a) Handling and storage of timber frame components;
(b) Making frame watertight;
(c) Fixing of insulation to walls;
(d) Installation of services;
(e) Checking moisture content before vapour barrier and dry lining applied;
(f) Flexible brick ties and so on.

Manufacturing specification for use of the manufacturer of the timber frame

This must cover:

1 The species, grades, sizes and moisture content of timber permitted for the various elements of the frame – studs, plates, lintels, sheathing, etc.

2 Tolerences permitted in the overall size of components.

3 Nail and staple specification.

It might also cover the method of loading for delivery in order that they may be unloaded in the correct sequence. It should also be stated whether a fork lift truck is available on site.

Erection specification

This is produced by the designer of the timber frame and specifies the sequence of erection of the components and other relevant parts, the fixings to be used and any particular points regarding the erection drawings that need special attention.

Typical headings in an Erection specification could include:

1 Explanation of drawings, reference numbers on components, etc.

2 Explanation of how components are delivered – window frames already fixed or not, joists cut to length or not, architraves and skirtings in random lengths or not, etc.

3 Explanation of how each constructional element is fixed given in recommended constructional sequence (see Ch. 7).

4 Nailing schedule giving size, type and number or centres of nail or staple for each fixing.

Should the building owner entrust the whole of the work to one builder, that builder will either have his own consultants or he will approach a manufacturer for a complete design service who will produce the manufacturing specification. He will also either produce an erection specification or include in his price to the builder for erecting the timber frame complete. In either case, the building owner would do well to check that the companies concerned are well experienced in this type of work and respected in the trade. Guidance from the local authority building inspector might be sought on this point.

Paying for the work by stage payments is probably best done by agreeing at the outset the percentage of the total contract sum payable at distinct stages of completion of sections of the work. Three such sections could be: slab completed ready for commencement of erection of frame; unit roofed in; and finally, unit ready for occupation. As an incentive for the builder to complete on time or sooner, every endeavour should be made to make the last instalment the most lucrative.

Large contract work such as housing estates

The building owner or estate developer will most certainly employ a designer, whether or not a qualified architect and whether an in-house employee or independent consultant. The designer will be responsible for the design of the whole contract, albeit he may seek the advice of consultants on such matters as foundations, roads and sewers, and timber frame superstructures. As far as the timber frames are concerned, the procedure is as for the individual unit except that tenderers will need to be told the required sequence of build, and the suppliers, or subcontractors, of the timber frame components will need to know the exact delivery programme required by the contractor.

A quantity surveyor may be employed to produce Bills of Quantities for the whole of the work to enable truly competitive tenders to be obtained. When this is the case, it is strongly advised that the supply and fixing of the timber frames should be treated as lump sum items per unit type and not measured out in detail. Conditions covering ends, steps, staggers and connections between different house types in a terrace, can all be treated as addenda, i.e. addendum 1 could be an extra over price to cover for a 600 mm step between two type A houses. This lump sum could be extended to cover the whole of the superstructure. A lump sum price for each house type and for each condition based on the fully detailed drawings, manufacturing specification, erection specification and building specification can be used on a summary page in the Bills of Quantities covering the superstructures, i.e. so many type A

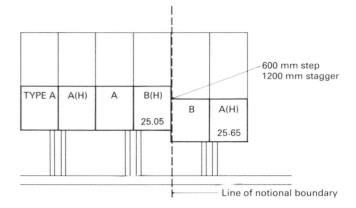

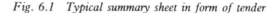

Summary sheet for such a scheme would be:

Type A	2 No. @ £	£
Type A handed	2 No. @ £	£
Type B	1 No. @ £	£
Type B handed	1 No. @ £	£
EO for left-hand end to Type A	2 No. @ £	£
EO for 600 step/1200 Stagger between type B and type B handed	1 No. @ £	£

EO = Extra over

Fig. 6.1 Typical summary sheet in form of tender

houses at so much plus so many addendum Bs at so much and so on (see Fig. 6.1).

Stage payments would have to be agreed per superstructure as explained for individual units. The advantages of this method are:

1 Saving on professional fees.

2 Incentive not to make variations. If variations are required, a price for them has to be agreed with the contractor before putting the variation in hand.

3 No provisional or pc (prime cost) sums.

4 Main part of contract at lump sum price not subject to remeasurement.

In addition to the tender documents set out for an individual unit, the following should be included for a tender for an estate:

1 Details of ends, steps, staggers and handings of individual units.

2 Details of planning permission and Building Regulation approval if granted.

3 Longitudinal and cross-sections of roads including sewers therein.

4 Complete setting-out drawing of houses and roads, footpaths, fences, etc.

5 Trees to be retained.

6 Landscaping required.

7 Details of trial holes if available or permission for tenderers to bore own trial holes.

8 Street lighting, substations and ducts in external works for electricity, gas, water, telephone and possible TV cables.

9 Responsibility for compliance with Section 18 and Section 38 agreements.

10 Precise details of phased hand-overs required.

These items may be further explained under the headings below.

Ends

If the housing estate includes terrace housing, it is normal for the superstructure of the house types to be drawn and taken off as intermediate units. Separate drawings and take-off schedules are prepared for left and right ends when looking at the drawn plan of the intermediate unit from the front. The end unit in a terrace will therefore always have an addendum condition. Care must be taken when an end condition applies to a handed unit on the layout. Although it might be a right-hand end on the layout, it will in fact be a left-hand-end addendum if it is handed to the way the intermediate unit is drawn (see Fig. 6.1).

Step

This is the difference in level between one house and the one adjoining. It is a great advantage to keep these as standard dimensions throughout a site. The differences between two levels forming the step could for example be 300, 600 or 900 mm over the whole site. A step of less than 300 mm is not very practicable because of the difficulty of flashing at the roof level, especially if there is a projecting barge-board on the roof of the higher dwelling. Steps of less than 300 mm can normally be overcome by grading ground levels.

Staggers

These occur where one unit projects in front of the one adjoining on plan. Again, if these can be kept to standard dimensions, i.e. not everyone different, it assists the taking-off and the operations on site.

Handings

The house types will probably be drawn to one hand only, yet the designer on the layout may show them as drawn and also handed to the drawing. The layout should be marked accordingly with a large letter H used to mark the handed units or in some other clear way. This has to be carefully watched on site and the manufacturer of the components must be made fully aware of the handed units before he commences manufacture. Handed units also affect the ordering of windows, external door frames, etc.

Planning permission

It is the contractor's responsibility to see that planning permission and Building Regulations approval have been obtained before commencing work on site. He should therefore be kept fully informed of the position with regard to these at the time of tender. References and dates of approvals received, or dates of applications made, should be the minimum of information given to tenderers.

Longitudinal and cross-sections of roads including sewers therein

These drawings will be in accordance with the local authority's own specifications and will form part of the Section 18 and 38 agreements if there are roads and sewers to be adopted by the local authority.

Complete setting-out drawings

With housing estates, it is preferable to prepare a grid over the whole site at say 10 m centres with each grid line referenced. Letters of the alphabet could be used for the horizontal lines and numbers for the vertical. Base points for the grid lines must be clearly shown and setting-out dimensions of individual units can then be shown from the nearest grid line.

Trees to be retained

As well as showing these on a drawing, it is advisable actually to mark the trunks of the trees with white paint on site. Provision should be made in the contract documents for the protection of the trees to be retained.

Landscaping

A clear and complete landscaping drawing should of course be produced, but provision must be made for separate completion dates and defects liability periods for landscaping as the work can only be carried out at certain times of the year and not necessarily to suit the contractor's programme of completions. A separate contract for landscaping, to commence after the hand-over of sections by the building contractor, is sometimes considered preferable.

Trial holes

Trial holes may have been dug before tenders are sought to enable the designer to have full information before designing the foundations, etc. In this case, they may be left open and protected to enable tenderers to inspect during the tenders period.

Sometimes a consultant is employed to produce a comprehensive report on soil conditions for the benefit of the designer. In this case, a copy of the report should be available to all tenderers. If no trial holes or report have been sought by the designer who sometimes shows depths of foundations diagrammatically and asks tenderers to provide foundations to a depth to suit the ground conditions and to the satisfaction of the local authority, then the tenderers should be allowed to bore their own trial holes during the tender period. Full details as to when this can take place, whom to contact and specification as to method, protection and making good, must be given to all tenderers.

Services

All details that the designer has obtained from the service authorities during the design stage are of great help to the tenderers. Existing services on the site are of paramount importance including overhead cables. Proposed runs of service mains, including ducts required across roads and footpaths, are also essential.

Section 18 and 38 agreements

'Power of local authority to agree to adopt sewer or drain, or sewage disposal works, at future date' is defined by Section 18 of the Public Health Act 1936. 'Power of highway authorities to adopt by agreement' is defined by Section 38 of the Highways Act 1980, Chapter 66.

These agreements are normally between the building owner or developer and the local authority. They cover the adoption of the public roads, footpaths, open areas, etc. and the main sewers. The agreements may include for maintenance periods quite different from those contained in the main contract and the responsibility of taking over these works normally rests with the local authority and not with the supervising officer of the contract. These points must be clarified in the tender documents. It must be made quite clear as to whose responsibility it is to get these works taken over by the local authority and whether or not these works are subject to the defects liability period in the contract as well as the maintenance period of the Section 18 and 38 agreements.

Phased hand-overs

The developer or building owner should clearly state in the tender documents which part or parts of the works he needs completing first. If he is of open mind on this point he should say so. He should, however, state the minimum number of units he is prepared to take over at any one time. Rather than put a number to this requirement, it is best to study the site plan and mark it up in phases to ensure that when a phase is handed over, access to the properties is available with the least inconvenience to the occupiers while the contractor completes the remaining phases. On large sites, discussion with the service authorities is essential before deciding on the phases for hand-over. It is no use contemplating completions from one end of the site if the electricity, for example, comes into the site from the other end. Agreement must be reached with all the service authorities.

An example of an alternative type of tender call

The examples quoted above can, of course, be modified in many ways according to the client's and designer's wishes and custom. The examples are given in some detail so that whatever method is adopted, the examples can at least act as a check-list to ensure that nothing is omitted from the tender documents. An alternative method recently encountered was as follows.

The client, a financier, bought a large site on which he wished to build houses to rent to the United States Air Force. The USAF produced very detailed performance specifications as to their requirements in the way of accommodation. Number of units, sizes of units, minimum room sizes, insulation values, standard and size of finishes, equipment, etc. The client employed an architect to design the scheme, obtain planning permission and Building Regulations approval; a consultant to design the timber frames and prepare schedules and specifications of the whole of the superstructures and a quantity surveyor to prepare a specification for the whole of the works, the contract conditions, agree stage payments and agree the final account.

At the commencement of the work on site, the client appointed a supervising officer to administer and supervise the contract.

Competitive tenders were obtained from selected contractors. At the time of tender, they were issued with the quantity surveyor's specification which included the local authority's specification for roads and sewers and the consultant's specification for the superstructures, complete sets of drawings from the architect and consultant used in obtaining Building Regulation approval and full details of proposed contract document (amended JCT form) including phased hand-overs required, liquidated and ascertained damages, etc. Fixed price tenders were called for so that the accepted tender should be the amount of the final account. The tenderers were asked to submit either samples or catalogue illustrations with their tender to illustrate what they have included to comply with the specification for the fittings and fixtures. The drawings and specifications having been previously approved by both client and the USAF, when the tenders were received, the client had only to accept the price and the USAF only agree the details of the fittings and fixtures. The contractor appointed was not permitted to vary the drawings and specification for the superstructures but was to be responsible for the design of all other works 'to the satisfaction of the local authority and supervising officer' and could amend any of the architect's drawings subject to the same conditions. The contractor was also responsible for constructing the road and sewers in accordance with the Section 18 and 38 agreements and being responsible for them until the end of their own individual maintenance periods.

The lowest tender was accepted and the contract proceeded to completion with no problems arising. The 300 houses complete with all roads and sewers were occupied within 67 weeks (see Fig. 7.2, p. 66) from starting on a virgin field and are illustrated in Fig. 6.2. The final account was virtually the accepted tender with the one provisional sum adjustment. One provisional sum had to be inserted due to a last-minute adjustment to a site access road before the contract commenced. However, the cost of the work to be set against the provisional sum was agreed before the particular part of the work commenced.

The final account was agreed and signed before the expiration of the defects liability period and the final release of retention was certified on the date of the final inspection at the end of the defects liability period.

Tenders generally

Generally recommendations regarding calling tenders may be summarized as follows:

1 Only invite contractors who are experienced in the type of work proposed.

2 Send out letters inviting contractors to tender long before you are ready to despatch the tender documents giving the contractors the approximate size of the job, the location, the dates and length of the tender period and the date of commencement on site.

3 Include with the tender documents as much useful information as possible taking care to ensure that any duplicated information is not in conflict.

Fig. 6.2 FrameForm timber frame housing in East Anglia for occupation by USAF personnel. Architect, John Alderton and Associates. Main Contractor, French Kier Construction Ltd.

4 Allow a reasonable time for the tenders giving ample time to the tenderers to obtain reasonable quotations for the work. If the tenderers are to be responsible for the design of any part of the work, the tender period must reflect this additional work. A short tender period means that the contractors tendering are going to have to take short-cuts and then cover themselves because of this. It is generally worth while giving tenderers ample time as it saves money in the end. If tenders are called during the winter period, it is very often seen that after a tender has been accepted in say January, work cannot start on site until March because of weather conditions. From this it will be seen that nothing would have been lost, but possibly something would have been gained, by allowing the tenderers another month in which to tender.

Chapter 7

Site erection

Delivery of components

Manufacturers and suppliers of component parts have various methods of delivery to sites. The one-off house will usually come complete on one load. With large contract work, manufacturers tend to stack panels horizontally in half-house sets, i.e. one set comprising all ground-floor panels, another all first-floor panels, etc. A half-house set of a normal three-bedroom house makes a convenient load for a fork lift truck to facilitate loading and unloading. The usual articulated lorry will carry a load at least two half-houses high, the total number carried being dependent on the length of the trailer. The important thing is to ensure that deliveries are made in the order required. A strongly advocated method is one whereby ground-floor panels are erected for quite a few houses before first-floors panels are delivered. This enables joists and floor decks to be constructed after the first ground-floor panels are up and the first-floor panels, when they arrive, may be placed on the first-floor deck of the appropriate units. This sequence, if carefully planned, will eliminate double handling of panels, i.e. straight from lorry to first-floor deck rather than from lorry to storage and then from storage to position for erection.

It is not advocated that the whole of the first-floor panels be placed in one stack on the first-floor platform by fork lift truck straight off the trailer. This causes great congestion in a limited space, as the panels then have to be sorted and placed in their correct positions. With small-panel construction, all panels are capable of being manhandled and can easily be lifted to the first-floor platform individually by hand and placed in position. On a good level site, it is sometimes possible to get the trailers alongside the ground-floor construction to enable panels to be lifted direct from trailer to first-floor location. In long terrace construction it might be found advantageous to lift the first-floor panels of the first house on to the floor deck of the adjoining house and so on along the terrace. This method overcomes the problem of congestion mentioned above.

Storage and handling of components on site

If panels have to be stored on site before erection, care must be taken to see that they are kept off the ground and level. It is preferable to have an external panel, with its sheathing uppermost, on top of the stack of panels if they are stacked horizontally. This will offer some protection from rain although, on a well-organized site, components should not be stacked on site for any length of time before erection. However, a sheathed external panel with the plywood facing downwards should never be placed on top of a stack of components, enabling rainwater to collect and be retained between the studs.

Joists

Floor joists should be kept well off the ground by use of cross-bearers at sufficient intervals to avoid sagging. If covered for protection from rain and sun, enough air must be allowed to circulate beneath the covers to permit the timber to breathe. It is prudent to remember that hot sunshine can cause as much, if not more, damage to kiln-dried timber than rain. Rainwater does not penetrate very deeply into timber and soon dries out, provided it is well ventilated and not allowed to remain submerged in water.

For comparatively small additional cost, floor joists can be banded together in house or block sets. This can be a great help on site and saves many man-hours sorting joists into sets. If house or block sets are used, they must never be allowed to be broken open except for use on the particular house or block. If one joist is borrowed for the house adjacent and so on, the benefits of having individual sets are soon lost. On large sites, it is recomended that spare sets for each house type be kept in the compound and used as replacements for any defective joists found in the sets out on site.

Roof trusses

Roof trusses should always be carried, stored and hoisted in an upright position. They should be stored with bearers at right angles under the same points at which they are supported when in position on the roof. No part of the truss should be touching the ground and protection should be afforded against rain and sun, as for joists. Simple stands made up from scaffolding are ideal for storage of trusses.

Trusses are usually delivered to site in bundles, strapped tightly together with metal or strong plastic straps. The metal connecting plates on trusses, being face-fixed, mean that the thickness of a bundle of trusses is greatest at the point of the plates. Therefore, the straps should go round the trusses in close proximity to the plates. If they are put round at mid-span, between plates, the timbers are drawn close together, causing distortion, especially to the outside trusses of the bundle. Such distortion will remain in the trusses when erected, causing problems for the roof tiler and ceiling tacker. In any case, the straps should be released as soon as the trusses are off-loaded on site and stored correctly, to prevent their cutting into the timber should the timber swell.

Trusses should always be manufactured with a slight upward camber in the ceiling joist. This is to allow for the slight deflection in the ceiling joist when the roof is loaded out. In this way, no load is put on the internal first-floor partitions which, generally, are not designed to be load-bearing. Trusses are normally designed to span from external wall to external wall. If the specification calls for the trusses to be nailed to the top of any internal partitions they cross, this should only be done after the roof is loaded and the deflection in the trusses has taken place. After loading, the trusses should then be just touching the tops of the internal walls they cross.

The mechanical plated truss has the prongs of the plates hydraulically pressed into the face of the timbers to secure the joint. It stands to reason, therefore, that any whip action activated in the truss will tend to weaken the strength of the joint. Indeed, if sufficient whip is put into the truss, the plates can be sprung out of the timber. The handling of trusses is, therefore, of paramount importance. If they are treated like a sheet of plate glass, all will be well.

Plywood

External quality plywood, when delivered in bulk, comes in packs of forty sheets, normally protected with a cover of thin plywood and tightly bundled with metal straps. These packs store well externally but if they are stored on site for any time, the metal straps should be cut. This enables the plywood to swell under atmospheric conditions without the straps cutting into the edges of the sheets, so causing damage, especially to the tongues and grooves. Adequate bearers to avoid contact with the ground are, of course, essential.

Erection of components

Before commencement of erection it is worth while to ensure that the sole plates are swept clean, that they are fixed adequately and completely bedded and that the overall dimensions are accurate.

The team of erectors should be equipped with claw hammers, boxed-out nail pouches round their waists, measuring tapes, level, step ladders, full set of drawings and specifications and an adequate supply of nails. A large magnet pulled over the floor by a piece of string will save a lot of back-bending and time in recovering dropped nails.

When panels are jointed together, they should be stitch-nailed, i.e. nails driven in at opposite angles on either side of the two members being nailed together.

Erection of components should commence with two panels forming an external corner and should continue in both directions until an internal wall panel is reached that meets the externals at right angles. At least one of these internal panels should be erected to assist bracing the externals before the internal panels are erected as a whole. If, in a particular design, there is a long length of external wall without an internal wall at right angles, some form of temporary bracing may be required until the whole structure is plumbed and completed.

On completion of the ground-floor components, including final plumbing and nailing, the top plates have to be secured. The fixing nails should never be driven straight into the timber, always at an angle (skew-nailed) and always staggered down the length of timber to avoid the possibility of splitting.

If the design calls for a straight flight internal staircase, ensure that it can be installed after the structure is up. Some designs, especially those with a straight flight staircase in the middle of the ground floor at right angles to the side walls, do not allow this, in which case the staircase must be installed with the ground-floor components.

Floor joists generally arrive on site cut to length. They are laid out on a module to suit plasterboard and plywood dimensions. Unlike in traditional construction, when the ends of floor joists meet over a load-bearing wall, the ends are butted together and 'scabbed' or faced with a piece of plywood or metal nailed truss plate to assist in keeping the two ends in the same plane. If the joists were to overlap each other as in traditional construction, they would obviously go off module.

As in all forms of good construction, any crown in the joists should be uppermost. If the specification calls for joists to be 'toe-nailed' into the top plates, great care must be taken to avoid splitting the edges of the joists. Galvanized metal joist clips are now readily available to avoid the need for toe-nailing.

Sometimes, designers will incorporate flitch lintels into the design of the floor in order to cope economically with wide spans and maintain a flush ceiling line. A flitch lintel can span at right angles to floor joists which will hang on either side by means of joist hangers. The flitch lintel will probably be formed of two joists bolted together, with a steel plate between the two. As the depth of the joists will inevitably shrink, it is important to see that the depth of the steel plate is less than the joist depth and that the timber oversails the steel top and bottom.

Ground-floor components must be plumbed and temporarily braced where necessary before the floor deck is applied.

Tongued and grooved sheet material for floor deck must be always be laid at right angles to the floor joists and annular-ringed shank nails used for its fixing. A complete pack of forty sheets of plywood should never be lifted and placed in one stack on the floor joists before fixing as the weight would exceed the floor design load.

First-floor panels and top plates are erected as for the ground floor. It might, however, prove advantageous to leave one external window panel unfixed to facilitate passing up the roof trusses by hand, keeping them vertical. The first end of the truss can be placed on the top plate of the opposite wall and the other end lifted on to the top plate adjacent to the omitted window panel. Still in an upright position, the trusses can then be stacked to one side of the opening, pending spacing and fixing after the window panel and top plate have been fixed. A window panel is recommended because the opening provides the facility for the erector to locate the last panel by leaning through the opening and tapping it into position from the outside. Some contractors find they can pass up the roof trusses through the cavity of the party wall. The spacing of the trusses can easily be marked on the top of the top plates or a spacing stick can be used. A pre-nailed temporary batten should also be marked with the correct spacing and used near the apex of the trusses to see that they are keep upright. Before final fixing of roof trusses and all specified bracing, a check should be made to ensure that any cold-water storage tank or storage platform specified will, in fact, pass through the proposed ceiling hatch. If it will not, then it must be inserted in the roof space before the final truss is fixed. For ease of working, it is strongly recommended that tank supports, etc. in the roof space be fixed before roof tiling.

Flat roofs

Flat roof construction is achieved in exactly the same way as intermediate floor construction except that falls to the sheet material are provided by placing firring pieces of timber on top of the joists. With cold deck flat roof construction, there are two important points to remember. Firstly, the space between roofing joists must be well ventilated to the outside air if the insulation is between the joists. If joists run at right angles to the external wall, each and every joist should be drilled in the header joist centrally between supporting joists or in the eaves soffit if there is an eaves overhang. If the joists run parallel to the external wall, each and every joist should be drilled in the neutral axis at, say, 600 mm centres or as specified by the designer. This is essential to enable the flat roof timbers to breathe, as they will normally be covered on the underside by an impervious vapour barrier and on the top side by an impervious roof covering. The importance for all structural timber to be allowed to breathe is covered elsewhere. Secondly, if a parapet wall surrounds the flat roof, the upstand of the flat roof covering material must be covered with a counterflashing. This must come down from the parapet in such a manner as to allow for the upstand to slide down behind the flashing when the roof joists shrink, the upstand still remaining adequately covered by the flashing (see Fig. 4.7, p. 46).

Noggings, fire-stop blockings, etc.

Site-fixed noggings and blockings should be fixed immediately the panels are erected. The position of the blockings will be shown on the drawings as they are a requirement of the Building Regulations, but noggings will have to be located according to the fixing requirements of the kitchen fittings, sanitary fittings, electrical fittings, etc. Very careful liaison with all these trades is essential. On a large site, site management can benefit greatly by preparing their own nogging drawings showing the total requirement for each house type. Early consideration and determination of nogging positions are essential, as they must be nailed in position as the panels go up to avoid delays in commencement of following sequences. Insulation, for example, cannot be inserted in external wall panels until after the noggings are fixed.

It is also worth mentioning here that, although centres of studs, joists and trusses may all generally be set out at 600 mm, pre-cut noggings will probably have to be three different lengths because of the different thicknesses of the timber used for the three purposes. For example, studs might be 38 mm, joists 44 mm and trusses 35 mm. Standard noggings would, therefore, be 562, 556 and 565 mm in length to suit 600 mm centres. Care must be taken to keep these carefully identified and used only for the purpose intended. It has often been claimed by operatives on site that noggings were delivered too long and were having to be cut, until it was pointed out that stud noggings were being used for joists.

Making the shell weathertight

The timber frame having been erected, several trades can now be brought in to work concurrently to render the dwelling weathertight.

Roof tiler. Roof tiling can commence immediately scaffolding is erected.

Plumber. The plumber will need to erect the soil and ventilation pipe to enable the roof tiler to complete his work.

Glazier. The glazier can carry out his external glazing utilizing the scaffolding erected for the roof tiler.

Carpenter. The carpenter can hang the external doors.

Application of breather paper

Some designers rely on the external quality of the sheathing material to keep the main shell weathertight before the application of the cladding. This is not recommended because the sheathing material is only butt-jointed and these joints can allow water penetration into the frames. Good practice timber frame construction is to cover the whole of the external face of the timber frame walls with a breather paper to form a moisture barrier. Breather paper is manufactured in rolls like roofing felt and is stapled to the sheathing in horizontal layers, starting at the bottom of the house and lapping each course, top over bottom, by at least 100 mm. The bottom run of breather paper should be extended downwards to protect adequately the exposed edge of the sole plate beneath the external components.

A hammer-type stapler has proved to be the best instrument for fixing breather paper but great care must be taken to avoid random stapling. It is important that the staples coincide with the staple or nail fixings in the sheathing material, that is, through the sheathing and into the studs. If this is carefully carried out as the breather paper is unrolled round the unit, it facilitates location and fixing of brick ties, battens for cladding fixings, etc. so that nails go through into the studs. That is to say, fixing nails for brick ties and battens are located over staples in breather paper and staples in breather paper are located over fixings in sheathing material which, in turn, are fixed into the studs.

The breather paper, or moisture barrier as it is sometimes known, must be a breather-type building paper conforming to BS 4016 : 1966. Although providing a barrier to keep moisture out of the timber frame from the outside, it does allow moisture under pressure from the inside to pass and the timber frame to breathe through it. Its function, therefore, is to protect and weatherproof the house immediately after erection of the shell and to provide a secondary line of defence against the penetration of wind-driven rain or moisture which may find its way through the exterior cladding materials, while allowing the escape of any moisture vapour which finds its way through the inner barrier or which is residual in the timber framing. Recent research has also indicated that when properly applied it also acts as a barrier to the passage of air from the exterior to the interior of the building.

If the timber frame shells are left for some time just wrapped in the breather paper before claddings are applied, damage to the breather paper can be caused by winds, especially on exposed sites. It is, therefore, essential to use a robust breather paper and ensure that it is adequately stapled. Some success is being achieved at the moment by stapling the breather paper through a narrow band of plastic tape. Besides assisting in keeping the staples in a straight line, it prevents the staples from pulling through the plastic tape as easily as they do through the breather paper. Cheap breather paper and inadequate stapling is a false economy.

Some designers have breather paper applied in the factory to each individual panel. When this is done, extra care must be exercised in handling the components to avoid tearing the breather paper and to ensure that cover strips are site applied to all joints, properly lapped top over bottom. Fixing the cover strips can hide the true line of staples, masking the position of studs for fixing purposes, which is another disadvantage of factory-applied breather paper.

Recommended nailing schedule for site erection

90 × 3.35 mm plain round

Sherardized or galvanized. To BS 1202 : Part 1 : 1974. Table 1.

Panels to sole plate	400 mm centres
Panels to floor deck	400 mm centres
Top plates to panels	600 mm centres
Header joists to external and separating wall	Toe-nailed to top plate at 600 mm centres
Joists, joist blockings or header joists meeting at 90°	Two nails at each junction driven into end grain through adjoining section
All 38 × 89 mm noggings	Two nails through each stud into end grain of nogging
Joist end on internal wall or separating wall	One nail toe-nailed into top plate
Joist or joist blocking passing over panel and joist blocking to separating wall	Two nails toe-nailed into top plate
Joist running along top of internal, external or separating wall	Toe-nailed into top plate at 600 mm centres
Panel to panel	Six nails to each joint – three to each side of studs to be joined – stitch-nailed
Roof trusses to top plates when truss clips are not used	Two nails each joint, toe-nailed to top plate preferably through holes in metal truss plate
Gable ladder to roof truss	600 mm centres along rafters and two nails where each rung crosses spandrel
Ceiling, rafter and web bracing to trusses	Two nails at each crossing point
All other fixings of timber to timber	

30 × 2.0 mm annular-ringed shank

Sherardized or galvanized. To BS 1202 : Part 1 : 1974 Table No. 21.

12.7 mm single layer of plasterboard	225 mm centres

45 × 2.65 mm annular-ringed shank

Sherardized or galvanized. To BS 1202 : Part 1 : 1974. Table No. 21.

Plywood floor deck to joists	150 mm centres along all edges and 300 mm centres along intermediate supports
Metal ties to separating walls	Two per tie
Any site fixing of sheathing to external panels	100 mm centres along edges and 300 mm centres over intermediate supports
Second of two layers of 12.7 mm plasterboard	Double nailed at 225 mm centres
19 mm plasterboard to separating wall	225 mm centres
19 mm plasterboard to ceilings	150 mm centres

50 × 2.0 mm annular-ringed shank

Sherardized or galvanized. To BS 1202 : Part 1 : 1974. Table No. 21.

12.7 mm plasterboard over 19 mm plasterboard	Double nailed at 225 mm centres

60 × 2.65 mm annular-ringed shank

Sherardized or galvanized. To BS 1202 : Part 1 : 1974. Table No. 21.

12.7 mm third layer of plasterboard to ceilings as used in construction of compartment floors	Double nailed at 225 mm centres

25 × 3.0 mm extra large head clout

Sherardized or galvanized. To BS 1202 : Part 1 : 1974. Table No. 4

Fixing cavity barriers	

40 × 3.75 mm square twisted

Sherardized or galvanized. To BS 1202 : Part 1 : 1974. Table No. 17.

Joist clips and joist hangers	Fill all holes
To scab plates over butt ends of joists	Two nails to each joists end

30 × 3.35 mm plain round

Stainless steel or sherardized or galvanized masonry nails.

Sole plates to anchors	800 mm centres

38.3 × 2.97 mm annular-ringed shank
Stainless steel.

| Brick ties to timber external walls | Two nails per tie |

³⁄₈ × ³⁄₈ in. crown × 18 gauge rust-resisting staples

| Securing insulation and vapour barrier | 150 mm centres along lines of studs and rails |

³⁄₈ × ³⁄₈ in. crown × 24 gauge stainless-steel staples

| Breather membrane to external panels | 150 mm centres along lines of studs and rails |

Note: By using 90 mm long nails to join two pieces of 38 mm thick timber enables an inspector easily to see that the right nails have been used in the correct way. Even when stitch-nailed, the driven ends should protrude from the far face.

Documentation required on site

In addition to the normal site documentation – site diary, programme of works, copy orders, etc. – the following documents are required specifically for timber frame construction.

Foundation details

These should include overall slab dimensions and diagonal dimensions as accuracy is essential to ensure accurate and easy construction of the timber frame.

Layout drawings

These should be adequately dimensioned preferably using a grid system, and should clearly indicate which units are handed, levels of each slab and different levels if the slab contains a step, and dimensions of staggers. If the same house type recurs on the site but with different claddings, the layout drawings should show the different claddings by using a code such as type 1A–a type 1 with all brick cladding and type 1B–a type 1 with tile hanging to first floor over brickwork to ground floor and so on.

Erection sequence drawings

These will show the positions of each part of the timber frame content of each unit.

Designer's erection guide

This may be in the form of notes attached to the erection drawings, notes issued on separate sheets of paper or sometimes in the form of an erection manual.

Nailing schedule

Can be a separate document, included in the designer's erection guide or just notes on the erection drawings.

NHBC Manual and Practice Note No. 5

Essential when houses are built under the NHBC guarantee scheme.

Plumbing and electrical layout drawings

Approved by the designer as mentioned in Chapter 3.

Superstructure specification

This should specify all the fittings, fixtures and finishings inside and outside the timber frame.

Manufacturing drawings and specification

The information given to the manufacturer of the timber components and supplier of loose timbers, must be available on site to enable the site staff to check that what they receive is in accordance with what has been ordered. The information must include precise sizes and tolerances permissible, moisture content, species and grades of timber and nailing requirements.

Inspection procedures

Generally speaking, too much supervision is not possible. This of course applies more to the contractor who has no previous timber frame experience than to those who are experienced. Even so, the experienced timber frame contractor will know that work generally proceeds much faster on a timber frame site than it does with traditional construction and unless there is adequate supervision at all stages of progress, inaccurate work and sometimes omissions can be overlooked causing expensive consequences at a later date. As a minimum, the following stages for inspection are suggested. Each stage should be approved by a foreman or clerk of works before the work is allowed to proceed to the next stage.

After fixing of sole plates

See that overall dimensions, including diagonals, are accurate. See that sole plates are accurately nailed and adequately packed where necessary. See that the sole plates are laid out in accordance with the house plan. Pay particular attention to handed units where the sole plates should be a mirror reflection to those shown on the drawings for the 'as drawn' house.

Before fixing of floor deck

Check nailing of ground-floor panels, floor joists and blockings. Check for ground-floor panels being plumb and true.

Before roof tiling

Check for structure being plumb and true. Check adequacy of nailing of first-floor panels and roof trusses. Particularly check all roof truss bracing – not only that the right bracing is in the right place but that the nailing is in accordance with the instructions. Check that the water storage tank and platform are in position.

Before commencement of applying insulation to inside of external walls

See that the shell is watertight with breather paper properly applied, roof covered in, windows glazed or at least covered in, and external doors hung. See that all noggings are in place and first-fix plumbing and electrical work is complete.

Before commencement of applying internal vapour barrier and plasterboard tacking

Check moisture content of timber frame and ensure that it is 20 per cent or below before allowing the next stage to proceed. It is suggested that random checks be made to bottom rails of ground- and first-floor panels, bottom edge of floor joists and to studs around window and door openings.

Generally

As will be seen from the nailing schedule, quite a few different types and size of nail are used in timber frame construction. This is, of course, not without reason although not always appreciated by the workmen on site. Constant supervision must always be given to the type, size, number or centres, how driven, etc. of all nails in timber and plasterboard and all staples in the breather paper and vapour barrier.

A careful watch must be kept at all times to see that floor joists are not overloaded with stored plasterboard as mentioned in Chapter 3. Tacked plasterboard to walls not to be in contact with floor deck – see also Chapter 3.

Ensure that the shrinkage gap between top of masonry and underside of timber is maintained in every case.

It is, of course, important to see that everything is carried out in accordance with the designer's instructions, but in this section faults that frequently occur in practice have been highlighted for special attention.

Inspectors must never forget when checking the size of timber that they must always also check the moisture content. The two must always go together.

Both the British Woodworking Federation (BWF) and NHBC have printed very useful check-lists for supervisors.

Sequence of building

To obtain the full benefits of building timber frame housing it has to be realized and appreciated that the sequence of building is quite different from that of traditional construction. A whole new approach is needed by those responsible for programming and construction. More careful planning and organization are required to see that the right materials and men are in the right place at the right time. If this is achieved, quite remarkable results can be obtained.

Man-hours

The calculation of man-hours required to erect the timber frame of a two-storey three-bedroom house, i.e. ground-floor panels, top plates, floor joists, plywood floor deck, first-floor panels, top plates and roof trusses, is a first essential to any programme. A rough guide is one man per two-storey three-bedroom house per working week. After a short learning curve, this can normally be improved upon and it will be found that four men can erect five such houses in a week. These

are superstructures only. In other words, it is after the foundations, ground-floor slab, sole plates and screed are ready to receive the superstructure.

Erectors normally work in gangs of three or four, but on large contracts it sometimes works out that one gang of three or four will erect all the ground-floor panels, top plates and joists, followed by a second gang who fix the plywood floor deck, first-floor panels, first-floor top plates and roof trusses. Very large contracts can be subdivided even further, so that a gang of, say, two men do nothing other than fix floor joists and become remarkably skilled and fast in the operation. Balancing these subdivisions, to gain a steady progressive flow of completed structures, needs careful watching and will vary according to the complexity of the design. Steps, staggers, projections and recesses on plan, bay windows, etc. all need additional thinking and additional work. They therefore take additional time.

Sequence of operations

Given that the ground-floor slab is complete up to sole plate and screed, the sequence of operations to follow for a two-storey three-bedroom house is generally as follows (operations listed against the same sequence number should be carried out simultaneously):

1 Ground-floor panels.
2 Ground-floor top plates.
3 Floor joists.
4 Floor deck.
5 First-floor panels.
6 First-floor top plates.
7 Roof trusses and gable ladders.
8 Soil and vent pipe.
   Fascias and rainwater gutters.
   Roof tiling.
   External doors.
   External glazing.
   Breather paper.
9 First-fix plumbing and electrical work.
   External cladding and rainwater down pipes.
   External painting (unless painter is prepared to work from ladders which is possible when windows are prefinished in the factory).
10 Dismantle scaffold.
   Insulation and vapour barrier.
11 Plasterboard tacking, tape and fill.
12 Second-fix carpenter, plumber and electrician.
13 Painting and decoration internally.
14 Floor coverings.

Brick chimney breast

If the design incorporates a brick-built chimney breast and flue, it is strongly recommended that this be accurately located on the slab and built at least up to first-floor level before the timber frame erection is commenced. Where a large breast stops at the underside of the ground-floor ceiling, care must be taken to see that the brickwork stops at least 10 mm below the underside of the floor joists to allow for the shrinkage of timber. No part of the timber frame should be built in contact with the brickwork.

Main differences from traditional counterpart

The sequence set out above will obviously vary slightly according to various conditions, size of contract and claddings to be used. However, it does highlight the main differences between the sequence of trades employed on timber frame housing. If a gang of four erectors is employed it will be seen that bearing in mind the rough calculation given earlier, from the commencement of erecting superstructures (stage 1), it is only a week before scaffolding for four dwellings is required (stage 8), and that is assuming four men only erect four houses in a week. This is the first apparent major difference from building traditionally; the short time from commencement until full scaffolding is required to enable the roof tiler to begin work. There would appear to be no statutory safety regulations at the moment specifically covering timber frame erection without scaffolding. It can, therefore, be assumed that the timber frame erector accepts the hazards of his trade as do steeplejacks, structural steel frame erectors and scaffolders. Not all safety officers share this view and early consultation with the local safety officer before commencement on site is strongly advised. Views and interpretation of the regulations vary tremendously up and down the country.

The glazier also carries out his work at a much earlier stage than in traditional construction.

It will be appreciated that, on completion of stage 9, the dwelling is completely sealed and weathertight, enabling all following trades inside the dwelling to work in dry and warm conditions. This is a great advantage to the man on site.

At the completion of stage 9, the dwelling is also structurally safe and sound since whatever cladding is used it is non-structural and in no way can be considered a structural element. Indeed, in Canada it is not unknown for a family to build its own timber frame house and begin living in it while it is still wrapped in breather paper, the claddings being added later as and when they can be afforded.

Scaffolding

The type and timing of scaffolding to be used are a very difficult thing to recommend as two experienced timber frame housing contractors seldom have similar ideas on the subject.

Small-panel platform frame construction (as opposed to large-panel construction requiring cranage to hoist it into position) can be erected without scaffolding. The problem arises when the dwelling has to be roofed, because roof tilers will not generally tile a roof unless full scaffolding is provided. It is interesting to note here that the only area in the UK where roof tilers have been found who did not insist on full scaffolding, was in Liverpool. There, the roof tilers were quite happy to work overhand from the inside and put the top course and ridge tiles on from ladders on the outside.

To erect full scaffolding at this stage (stage 8), could, if not carefully thought out, hinder work of subsequent trades, i.e. glazing, cladding, application of breather paper, etc. One of the ways commonly used to overcome this problem is to erect full scaffolding a short distance away from the timber frame and then use cantilevered brackets on the inside at various levels to suit the various trades. One experienced timber frame contractor finds it preferable to erect scaffolding for the roof tiler, then dismantle and re-erect as cladding rises. However, the cantilevered bracket system seems preferable to, and certainly more economical than, this duplicate system.

There are now available to timber frame contractors various forms of hanging scaffold devised to provide scaffolding for the roof tiler which does not have to rise up from the ground (see Fig. 7.1). Hanging scaffold consists generally of an upright pole with a hook at the top and cantilevered brackets to receive scaffold boards. The hooked end is placed over the top-floor top plate and the pole rests against the outside of the top floor panel or is kept a short distance from the sheathing by means of spacers. The cantilevered brackets incorporate an upstand baluster to hold a handrail/guard-rail. On completion of the roof tiling, the supporting pole is

Fig. 7.1 Hanging scaffold in course of erection

unhooked from the wall panel from inside the dwelling by withdrawing a connecting pin or some such similar device. Various manufacturers have devised a number of patent hooks and connections to facilitate this dismantling operation.

While some contractors have used this system quite successfully, the drawbacks include: restricted walkway when the design includes a large eaves overhang; difficulty of operation with layouts involving steps and staggers between houses; impossibility of use at gable ends with pitched roofs; careful planning and spacing required to avoid window openings, projecting sills, SVPs inside external walls, etc.; and, where there are no internal partitions at right angles to the top-floor external panels, the hanging scaffold can bow out the external walls.

Summary of main differences in sequence of operations

To summarize, the main differences in sequence of operations that must be appreciated in order to achieve the full advantages are: scaffolding required on site within hours of commencement of panel erection; roof tiler to commence very soon after start of panel erection; and hanging of external doors and glazing of all openings required much earlier than with traditional construction.

Benefits to specialist trades

The well-organized site will find that plumbers, electricians, heating engineers, etc. will soon appreciate the benefits of working on a timber frame scheme where they are able to work in dry and comparatively warm conditions inside the weathertight structure. Another advantage not generally appreciated until experienced, is that men working inside the building on first fix are able to walk through internal walls (i.e. between studs) instead of having to walk further by having to use door openings as in masonry built structures. Similarly, in terraced housing, men are able to walk from house to house (i.e. between studs on the twin-leaf party wall) without having to go outside in possibly cold and wet conditions. Builder's work in connection with wiring and plumbing does not entail the need for a labourer to make holes through, and chases in, mansonry walls. All these advantages make timber frame more attractive to plumbing, heating and electrical trades. This fact alone can be advantageous to the contractor and his site operatives, especially during times of plenty of work and shortage of labour.

Controlled shell erection

On large sites, once shell erection commences, there is a great temptation to surge forward, putting up shells way ahead of following trades. On contract work, this is sometimes encouraged by terms of the contract, whereby the contractor is paid for materials as they are delivered. Contractors soon find that shell erections can produce quite large certificates of payment at an early stage of the job and so greatly assist cash flow. This must be resisted because to proceed too quickly with shell erection creates great management and supervision problems and spreads the site unnecessarily. It can also lead to many erected shells remaining unroofed for long periods leaving the timber exposed to the elements. This should be avoided at all costs. Ideally, shell erection should go no faster than the slowest trade following.

Storage conditions at the place of manufacture of the components are normally far better than the storage conditions available on site. Careful programming of deliveries is therefore essential to ensure that stacks of components do not litter the site awaiting erection. Besides the additional cost to the builder of double handling, unprotected stacks of components around the site create a bad psychological effect on the building owner and/or prospective purchaser. The aim must be to take delivery of the components, get them erected and covered in just as quickly as possible.

Case history of an actual contract

In order to prove that what has been written above is not all theory, the following facts are taken from the records of an actual contract successfully completed recently. The contract was for 300 units for occupation by USAF personnel on a farmland site in East Anglia (see Fig. 6.2, p. 56). The contract consisted of 128 three-bedroom houses, 172 two-bedroom flats, roads, sewers, play areas, pumping station and full landscaping. The houses were built in terraces of two, three and four while the flats were built in two-storey blocks of four flats each. Each block of flats had all facing brick cladding while the houses had facing bricks to all ground floors with either vertical timber siding or render to upper floors. All units had concrete roofing tiles to pitched roofs and were equipped to a high standard including fitted carpets to most rooms.

From date of possession to date of hand-over of last of 300 units was 67 weeks. This record of times is reproduced in the form of a bar chart in Fig. 7.2.

If comparison is made between the recommended sequence of operations and the actual record of progress on this particular site, it will be seen that they are remarkably close. However, a few points come to light. On this site the contractor chose to erect the wall panels without scaffolding but erected scaffolding before commencing with roof truss fixings. Plasterboard tacking commenced one week before glazing because there was, in fact, a slight delay in obtaining the sealed double glazing which delayed the start of this trade by 2 weeks.

The actual contract documentation was rather unusual but very successful. It is described in detail in 'An example of an alternative type of tender call' in Chapter 6, p. 55.

Actual recorded times of the various operations are:

	Week no. commenced	Week no. completed	Weeks taken to complete
Roads, sewers, foundations, etc.	1	36	35
Sole plates and screeds	12	36	24
Ground-floor components	13	38	25
First-floor components	14	39	25
Erect scaffold	14	42	28
Roof trusses	15	43	28
Roof tiling	15	46	31
Timber cladding	17	48	31
Carpenter 1st fix	17	47	30
Electrician 1st fix	18	48	30
Plumber 1st fix	18	49	31
Brick cladding	19	51	32
Glazing	21	52	31
Plasterboard tacking	20	54	34
Plasterboard tape and fill	22	56	34
Artex ceilings	22	56	34
Carpenter 2nd fix	24	59	35
Plumber 2nd fix	25	56	31
Electrician 2nd fix	25	65	40
Make good plasterboard	25	63	38
Drain connections	25	51	26
Water service	25	54	29
Electricity service and meters	26	66	40
GPO service	27	59	32
Garden paths and shed bases	27	65	38
Fencing	30	66	36
Wall tiles	25	63	38
Decorations	27	65	38
Garden sheds	28	65	37
Electric heating	29	67	38
Test services	30	65	35
Floor tiles	30	65	35
Bathroom accessories and carpets	30	67	37
Hand-overs	32	67	37

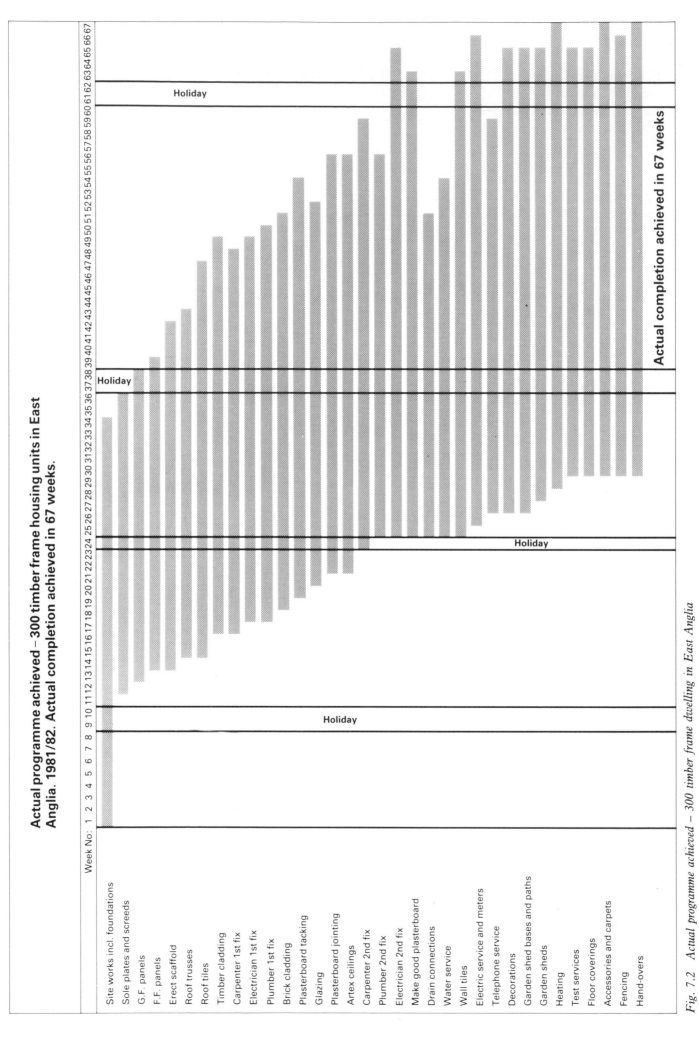

Fig. 7.2   Actual programme achieved – 300 timber frame dwelling in East Anglia

Chapter 8
Occupation of the timber frame building

Information for the purchaser

Some progressive housing developers provide for their customers a purchaser's guide book and pack on the day of occupation. The guidebook can contain such information as location of electrical fuses, water main stopcock, gas main stopcock, meters, etc.; names and addresses of nearest doctor, dentist, hospital, vet, post office, local authority, service authorities, etc. and a general description of the house and its construction. The pack accompanying the guide book can contain manufacturers' publications on the heating installation and all other appliances provided, fuse wire, a couple of electric light bulbs, a small screwdriver and even a toilet roll – all things likely to be welcomed by a new purchaser on moving-in day.

Currently, there is a move afoot to make compulsory the issue of a house log-book which would pass from original builder to first owner and then on to all subsequent owners, similar to the old log-book and present registration certificate that goes with a motor car. It is suggested that this log-book should contain the names and addresses of the builder and designer together with a detailed description of the construction. The relevant drawings would be attached together with the NHBC guarantee certificate where applicable.

A combination of the suggested log-book and the more domestic package mentioned previously, would indeed be a service to customers and provide an extremely good marketing point. Where this service is not provided, the prudent purchaser builds up his own file of information over the years which should be passed on when the house is sold.

Know your timber-framed building

With a timber-framed building it is essential that the occupier knows something of the construction and to realize that the walls are hollow needing special consideration when fittings and fixtures are to be secured to them. The problem of drilling and plugging holes in masonry walls does not exist but special techniques of fixing to hollow walls have to be adopted.

A range of fasteners specifically intended for stud walls is illustrated in Fig. 8.1. For light objects, such as lightweight picture frames, it is possible to use self-adhesive hooks. Heavier pictures may be hung from hooks fixed directly into studs, or if positioning between studs is desired, then a simple hook can be used in conjunction with a cavity toggle device.

Heavy objects such as wash basins fixed by the builder, will normally have been screwed into a timber nogging within the timber-framed wall. If an additional basin is required, a pedestal basin will relieve some of the load on the wall fixing as most of the load will be carried on the floor. Where a wall-mounted basin is necessary it should be screwed to a backing board which

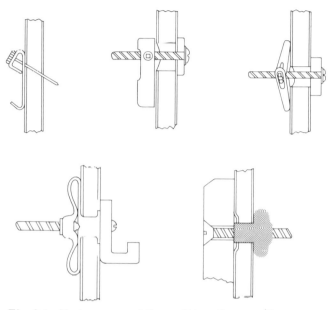

Fig. 8.1 Various patented fixture fittings for use with wallboards

in turn is large enough to be fixed through the plasterboard into at least two studs.

Wall cupboards will normally be wide enough to be screwed directly into the wall studs. Curtain rails can either be fixed directly into the timber lintels behind the plasterboard over windows where they exist or else a batten can be screwed into the studs over windows to receive the curtain rail.

Finding a stud in a timber-framed wall is a relatively simple matter and can often be accomplished by simply tapping the wall. Tap the wall from left to right until a more solid sound is heard. Mark the position and repeat the operation from right to left. A point midway between the two marks will be approximately over the centre line of the stud. A small magnet can be used to locate the plasterboard fixing nails in the studs and in North America a small gadget is marketed which works on the magnet principle. A small magnet is pivoted in a plastic dome so that when the dome is passed over the plasterboard, the pivoting magnet will move as it passes over the nails.

For large and heavy fittings, where noggings were not provided during construction, horizontal battens should be screwed into the studs through the surface of the plasterboard at the required heights to receive the heavy fittings.

Maintaining adequate ventilation

A modern timber-framed building represents the best of traditional building and building experience coupled with the advantages of modern building technology enabling the optimum use of currently available materials. As explained in Chapter 3, great care has been taken to prevent the moisture vapour created inside the building escaping into the timber structure causing interstitial condensation. Great care has also been taken to conserve energy by the introduction of insulation in walls and roof space, double glazing probably and tight fitting weatherproof doors and windows. However, up to 2 gallons of water vapour can be produced by a family of four in one house in a day and this has to go somewhere. Ventilation is the answer. Extract fans to bathrooms and kitchens, discharging to the outside air, are very desirable and clothes-drying machines must exhaust to the outside. On no account should fans and drying machines discharge into the roof space.

The presence of condensation on the inside of windows is the obvious sign that excessive water vapour is present and must be eliminated. Immediate ventilation can be obtained by simply opening the windows. Continued condensation on the inside of the glass will lead to water running down and causing unsightly deterioration and discoloration to the frames and sills and, if excessive, even to adjacent plasterboard.

Maintenance of timber-framed building

In addition to the normal maintenance inspections of a masonry-built structure – cracking in brickwork and render, blocked drains and gullies, blocked rainwater pipes and gutters, broken roof tiles, defective flashings, flaking and faded paintwork, blocked ventilation to roof space, etc., the following items for inspection are perhaps particularly important with regard to timber frame structures.

Externally, the ventilation holes or open vertical joints in brickwork need to be cleaned out and left clear in order that they may do the job for which they were intended – ventilate the cavity between the brick cladding and timber frame. The mastic or caulking around joinery needs to be regularly inspected and replaced where it has broken down and no longer provides an adequate and continuous seal.

Internally, the main difference between a timber-framed building and its masonry-built counterpart is with the internal lining, i.e. plasterboard dry lining as opposed to wet plaster. The absence of cracks appearing with timber frame construction is most noticeable. This is because the installation of the plasterboard linings in accordance with Chapter 3 has timber as a constant backing material. Plasterboard is fixed to timber walls, timber ceilings and timber lintels all having the same coefficient of expansion and contraction. In masonry construction, wet plaster is applied to many different backing materials – on plaster laths fixed to timber joists and roof trusses, blockwork, brickwork and concrete lintels – all with different coefficients of expansion and contraction. Because of this, these backing materials expand and contract differently according to atmospheric conditions, causing the cracking of the plasterwork where the two differing materials adjoin. Lintel cracks, where ends of concrete lintels meet brickwork or blockwork, and ceiling to wall joints where timber joists meet block or brick walls, are two common positions where plaster cracks are almost inevitable with masonry construction.

If nail popping occurs in the dry lining, another nail should be inserted about 50 mm above or below and the

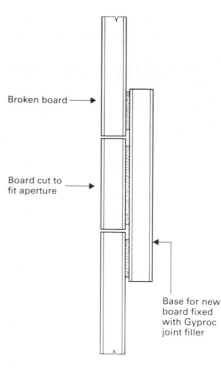

Fig. 8.2   Repair to large hole in dry lining

offending nail driven home and both spots made good with filler.

Plasterboard is a fairly robust material and is not easily damaged but should an indentation occur through accidental damage by moving furniture or the like, it can easily be remedied since plasterboard takes proprietary fillers readily without any elaborate preparations. A sheet of 12.7 mm plasterboard properly secured to frame elements with studs at 600 mm centres is certainly tough enough to withstand normal household wear and tear. Should, however, a hole occur in the plasterboard which is too large for repair with filler, the method for repair is as shown in Fig. 8.2.

Extensions and conversions to timber frame structures

It has become common practice for owners to modify or extend their home to adapt to changes in their living patterns or the size of their families. Many new homes are specifically designed to allow for future changes especially in the so-called starter homes. The shortage of residential building land puts a premium on maximizing the use of land and there is a great deal to be said for providing the facility, at the time of initial building, to expand into the roof space or garden areas. Where there has been no allowance for alteration or expansion and structural changes and Building Regulation approval are necessary, the services of a structural engineer or experienced timber frame designer will be required. If the house is relatively new, the owner should be able to obtain a copy of the original working drawings and the structural engineer's certificate from the builder. These will be of great help when designing extensions and conversions and avoid the need and cost of a survey of the existing property.

The use of clear span trusses often means that in bungalows and on the top floor of houses, none of the internal walls are load-bearing. They can therefore be removed or cut through without problem. Similarly constructed walls of the lower floors of buildings, might easily be load-bearing and the floor will need propping while an opening is cut through the wall and a lintel inserted. Professional advice should always be sort with this type of problem. If drawings are not available, the position of the wall in relation to the span of the floor joists will enable the professional to ascertain which walls are load-bearing.

If the building was constructed correctly originally and maintained correctly, after a year or more of occupation all the structural timber should be at 15–16 per cent moisture content. It is therefore essential to see that all structural timber used in extensions and conversions has a maximum of 16 per cent moisture content

to avoid differential movement between original and new.

Timber-framed buildings are relatively simple to build in the first instance and even more easy to extend or adapt. However, two very important points must always be borne in mind:

1 A hollow stud partition wall may be load-bearing. There is a common misapprehension that because it is a timber stud partition it cannot possibly be load-bearing and can therefore be removed. Disastrous results have occurred where this has been done.

2 In all cases of doubt or major alteration, consult an experienced designer or structural engineer.

Fig. 8.3   FrameForm timber frame houses and flats at Basildon, Essex, showing complicated roof design achieved. Architects: Basildon Development Corporation

Fig. 8.4   Timber frame house at Sunninghill by Wates Built Homes (Photograph by David Leech)

Fig. 8.5 Private development scheme in Rileyform timber frame construction

Fig. 8.6 Three-storey townhouses in timber frame

Fig. 8.7 Timber frame house at Newmarket (from The Heritage Range by Potton Ltd,)

Fig. 8.8   Timber frame house at Ascot (from The Heritage Range by Potton Ltd,)

Glossary of technical terms used

Angle bead Metal angle used to reinforce external wallboard angles.

Annular-ringed shank nail Nail with a rough or deformed shank making it difficult to withdraw (see Fig. A.1).

Bay window Window and floor which project beyond the main face of a building. When only the window frame projects, see Projecting window.

Blind nailing Nailing in such a way that the nail heads are not finally visible on the finished face.

Blockings Pieces of timber placed at right angles between joists or studs and of section the same size as the joists or studs.

Bottom rail Horizontal member of timber frame wall panel that sits on sole plate or floor deck.

Breather paper Material wrapped round external face of timber frame shell to keep moisture out of timber frame from the outside while allowing moisture under pressure to pass through it from the inside.

Brick veneer Half-brick-thick cladding to timber frame structure.

Building Regulations The Building Regulations 1985 and subsequent amendments, a statutory instrument published by Her Majesty's Stationery Office.

Butt joint Joint made by jointing two members together end to end without overlapping.

CLS Canadian Lumber Standards – stress graded, planed four sides, arrises rounded and in standard size sections. Some species of timber are always kiln-dried.

Cant strip Wedge or triangular-shaped piece of timber as used round perimeter of flat roof where it meets wall to avoid dressing roof covering material into a 90° angle. Also referred to as tilting fillet.

Cavity barrier Complete obstruction placed in cavity to prevent spread of flame and smoke. To prevent cavity acting as flue.

Cavity-fill slab Material used to form cavity barrier.

Ceiling brace Timber bracing battens on top side of ceiling chords of roof trusses.

Ceiling chord Bottom horizontal member of truss rafter to underside of which plasterboard is fixed to form ceiling to area directly below.

Cladding Non-structural material applied to outside of timber frame shell to give decorative and weatherproof finish.

Cold bridge Break in continuous insulation barrier caused by wall insulation which is cut short, leaving air space at top or bottom. Also caused by ceiling insulation which does not extend far enough to meet wall insulation.

Compartment floor Floor dividing units of accommodation within building.

Condition Term used to signify differences between houses on layout plan. Steps in level, staggers on plan and different houses joined together in a terrace all produce 'conditions'.

Contraction Shrinkage of materials due to atmospheric conditions, e.g. timber contracts when excessive heat applied, causing lowering of moisture content.

Counterflashing Flashing applied above another to shed water over top of under-flashing and to allow some differential movement to joint protected, without damage to flashing.

Cripple stud Shortened stud used in wall panel to support lintel over opening. It fits between top of bottom rail and underside of lintel.

Dressed timber Timber that has been planed on all four sides. Wrought timber.

Dry lining Interior wall and ceiling finish achieved by nailing plasterboard to frame and filling nail holes and joints with filler compound.

Dry wall Partition, separating wall or wall lining which used plasterboard as lining instead of wet plastering.

Edge The narrow side of sawn timber.

End grain Face of piece of timber exposed when fibres are cut transversely.

Expansion Enlargement of materials due to atmospheric conditions, e.g. timber expands when moisture content increases due to exposure to wet conditions.

Face Broad side of sawn timber.

Fire stops Fire-resistant material used in timber frame construction to prevent spread of flame from one building element to another.

Firring piece Piece of timber with one face tapered to provide sloping surface on top when laid flat on level surface, e.g. laid on top of joists to provide fall to flat roof.

Flitch beam or lintel Beam or lintel consisting of sandwich of two pieces of timber with steel core between them, all securely fastened together.

Floating floor Sound-deadening floor construction within each room resting on, but not secured to, structural joists. As used when constructing flats.

Floor deck Upper floor or platform on which upper-wall panels are erected.

Good one side Quality of plywood where knot holes are made good in finish of one side of each sheet.

Good two sides Quality of plywood where knot holes are made good to finish of both sides of each sheet.

Grading Classification of timber into established quality grades within the species.

Gypsum plasterboard Building board complying with BS 1230 : 1970. Composed of a core of aerated gypsum plaster bonded between two sheets of heavy paper.

Hair crack Crack just visible to naked eye.

Hanging scaffold Special scaffolding devised for timber frame construction provided by hooking brackets over top of uppermost wall panels. These brackets receive walkways and guard-rails. Brackets are dismantled externally after patent hooks are released internally.

Header Joist Joist at right angles to series of joists

where they terminate.

In stick Expression given to stacked timber which has battens at right angles at intervals up stack to allow free circulation of air to all timbers within stack.

Joist clips Metal fasteners used to secure ends of joists to top plates.

Joist hangers Metal fasteners used to secure two joists together at right angles at the same level.

kN/m² Kilonewtons per square metre. Unit of weight-to-area ratio used in calculating loadins on floors, foundations, etc. 1.5 kN/m² is the approximate equivalent of 30 1b/ft².

Ladder frames Simple frames nailed to end truss, cantilevered over spandrel panel to create roof overhang at gable ends.

Large-panel construction Form of platform frame construction where storey-height whole walls are made up as one panel, usually requiring lifting gear to hoist into position.

Lathing Building element fastened to frame of a structure to provide base for a rendered finish.

Moisture content Expressed as a percentage:
$$\frac{\text{Wt of moisture in timber}}{\text{Wt of oven-dried timber}} \times 100 \text{ per cent}$$

Moisture meter Small instrument used for measuring moisture content. Sensitive probes inserted into timber which give reading on a gauge.

Nogging Horizontal piece of timber fixed between vertical studs to provide solid fixing for fittings of all kinds.

Notching Cutting out small sections of edge of timber, usually to allow passage of pipes across timber at right angles.

Panels Units of wall construction – external wall panels, internal wall panels, window panels, etc.

Plumb Vertical. To make vertical

Projecting window Window frame only which projects beyond main face of building. If floor projects with window, it becomes a bay window.

Rafter bracing Timber bracing battens fixed to underside of roofing rafters of roof trusses.

Regularizing Defined in BS 4471 as process by means of which every piece of batch of constructional timber is sawn and/or machined to uniform width.

Reveal Visible part of each side of recess or opening in wall.

Roofing rafters Main angled timbers of roof truss to which roof covering is fixed.

Scabbing Expression used for fixing plate of metal or plywood to cover butt joints in floor joists.

Select sheathing Quality grade of plywood.

Separating wall Common wall separating two buildings. Also known as party wall.

Sheathing Quality grade of plywood. Sheet material used on outside of external wall panels.

Shell Erected timber frame structure complete, before following trades commence work.

Siding Cladding other than brick veneer, tile hanging or render.

Skew-nailing Nailing through side of one piece of timber at angle into face of another. Also known as toe-nailing and tosh-nailing.

Small-panel construction Platform frame construction where storey-height walls are made up of panels that can be manhandled and nailed to each other on site without use of mechanical equipment.

Soffit Exposed under-surface except ceilings.

Sole plates Timber members secured to foundations under all ground-floor wall panels.

Spandrel panels Wall panels with top rails at angle of the roof pitch. When placed on top of top-floor wall panels at ends of house or terrace, they form gable end.

Square twisted nail Nail with square section shank with twist in its length to prevent easy withdrawal (see Fig. A.1).

Standard (as used with timber measure) 165 cu ft of softwood. Now replaced by use of cubic metre.

Stick building Expression used when wall units are fabricated on site, i.e. panels are not prefabricated.

Stitch nailing Nailing two pieces of timber together by driving nails at opposite angles through each of the two exposed sides so that they cross at right angles to each other.

Stress grading Classification of timber into established quality grades within the species.

Studs Full height vertical members of all wall panels.

Suspended floor Any floor that does not have solid and complete bearing.

T & G Tongued and grooved.

Tacking Nailing plasterboard to timber frame.

Tape and fill Method of finishing tacked plasterboard by making good nail holes and covering joints with tape and filler compound.

Tapered-edge plasterboards Plasterboards with a wide bevelled edge along both long sides on face to facilitate tape-and-fill operation.

Template Pattern used as guide for setting out work.

Tilting fillet See Cant strip.

Toe-nailing See Skew-nailing.

Trimmer Joist alongside opening into which joists are framed.

Truss clips Galvanized metal fasteners nailed into top-floor top plates to receive and fix bearing positions of truss rafters.

Truss plates Galvanized metal plates that cover and hold together flush joints in timber prefabricated truss rafters. Held in position either by nails driven through pre-drilled holes in plates or projecting prongs on plates hydraulically pressed into the timber by various patented machines.

Truss rafters Prefabricated timber roof trusses usually designed to span between external walls and comprising roofing rafters, ceiling rafters and intermediate supporting webs and struts, all in the same plane, joints in timbers covered and secured by truss plates.

Vapour barrier Material used to prevent passage of water vapour or moisture.

Volumetric Method of construction where sections of building are finished complete in factory and have only to be hoisted into position on site, on to prepared foundations, and then joined together.

W/m² °C Watts per square metre per degree Centigrade, the unit used to measure heat loss through building elements (*U* value).

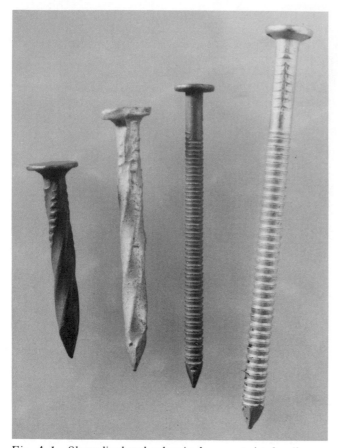

Fig. A.1   Sherardized and galvanized square twisted nails on left and sherardized and galvanized annular ring shanked nails on right

Appendix 2
Useful names and addresses

American Plywood Association, APA
European Division,
101 Wigmore Street,
London W1H 9AB
(01–629 3437)

British Gas Corporation,
152 Grosvenor Road,
London,
SW1   (01–821 1444)

British Gypsum Product Training Centre,
PO Box 6,
Erith,
Kent DA8 1BQ
(Erith 41122)

British Insurance Association, (BIA)
Aldermary House,
Queen Street,
London EC4
(01 248 4477)

British Standards Institution, (BSI)
2 Park Street,
London W1A 2BS
(01 629 9000)

British Wood Preserving Association, (BWPA)
Premier House,
150 Southampton Row,
London WC1
(01 837 8217)

British Woodworking Federation, (BWF)
82 New Cavendish Street,
London W1M 8AD
(01 580 5588)

Building Research Establishment, (BRE)
Garston,
Watford,
Hertfordshire WD2 7JR
(092 73 74040)

Building Societies Association, (BSA)
14 Park Street,
London W1A 2BS
(01 629 0515)

Chipboard Promotion Association, (CPA)
Stocking Lane,
Hughenden Valley,
Bucks. HP14 4NU
(0240 24 3091)

Council of Forest Industries of British
Columbia, (COFI)
Tileman House,
131–133 Upper Richmond Road,
Putney,
London SW15 2TR
(01 788 4446)

Dry Lining and Partition Association, (DLPA)
82 New Cavendish Street,
London W1M 8AD
(01 580 5588)

Fire Research Station, (FRS)
Boreham Wood,
Hertfordshire WD6 2BL
(01 933 6177)

Fibre Building Board Development Organization
Ltd. (FBBDO)
1 Hanworth Road,
Feltham, Middx.
(01 751 6107)

House-Builders Federation, (HBF)
82 New Cavendish Street,
London W1M 8AD
(01 580 5588)

National House Building Council, (NHBC)
Chiltern Avenue,
Amersham,
Bucks. HP6 5AP
(024 03 4477)

Solid Fuel Advisory Service,
Hobart House,
Grosvenor Place,
London SW1
(01 235 2020)

Southern Forest Products Association
and Western Wood Products Association,
69 Wigmore Street,
London W1H 9HB

Swedish–Finnish Timber Council, (SFTC)
21 Carolgate,
Retford,
Nottinghamshire DN22 6BZ
(0777 706615)

Timber Research and Development (TRADA)
Association,
Hughenden Valley,
High Wycombe,
Bucks. HP14 4ND
(0240 24 3091)

Timber Trades Federation (TTF)
Clareville House,
Whitcomb Street, London WC2H 7DL
(01 839 1891)

Index